ATLAS of the
UNEXPECTED

ATLAS of the UNEXPECTED

Haphazard discoveries, chance places
and unimaginable destinations

TRAVIS ELBOROUGH

MAPS BY **MARTIN BROWN**

WHITE
LION
PUBLISHING

CONTENTS

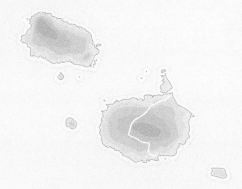

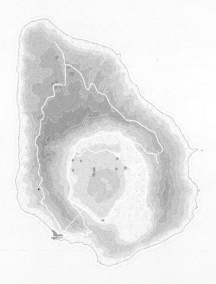

INTRODUCTION

In Greek mythology, Atlas is a Titan whose punishment for leading a revolt against the Olympian gods is to bear the weight of the heavens upon his shoulders. It was Gerardus Mercator, the foremost geographer of the Renaissance, who first applied the name to a collection of maps and charts. Born Gerhard Kremer, the son of a cobbler, Gerardus Mercator was the esteemed court 'cosmographer' to Duke Wilhelm of Cleve in Duisberg, Germany. Published in the spring of 1595, and four months after the mapmaker's own death at the age of eighty-two, his *Atlas, sive Cosmographicae meditationes de fabrica mundi* carried an illustration of the great Titan with the whole world in his hands on its frontispiece, accompanied by the statement, 'I have set this man Atlas so notable for his erudition, humaneness, and wisdom as the model for my imitation.'

Completed by Mercator's son, Rumold, and containing 107 maps – of which 102 described regions in Europe, but lacking charts of Spain and Portugal – Mercator's Atlas fell somewhat short of the full 'fabrick'd world' of its title. Its instigator had certainly intended to include detailed maps of all the other continents, but a series of strokes that left him partially paralysed and near blind had prevented him from achieving that ambition. Of the maps he did supply, those of 'The Arctic Lands' were largely works of fiction, with four islands around the North Pole and a landmass called Frisland, subsequently found not to exist – the latter, supposedly having been copied from an earlier fraudulent map by Nicolò Zeno, the fifteenth century Italian explorer suspected of faking most of his voyages. Mercator not only gave us the concept and name of the atlas, but his specific method of mapping opened up the world to all future globetrotting, by solving the problem of representing the spherical Earth on a flat piece of paper. So-called 'Mercator's projection' works by rendering parallels and meridians as straight lines that are mathematically spaced from the equator in such a way as to produce an accurate ratio of latitude to longitude that enabled mariners, in particular, to plot a course from one place to another with precision. This rigorously systematic cartography puts reality at the mercy of representation, stretching the northern and southern regions of the globe in order to keep the bearings orderly. One downside is that it warps the world in the Northern Hemisphere's favour, most famously resulting in a Greenland far vaster than either South America or Australia on world maps pinned to classroom walls across the globe. Its virtues – clarity and sheer navigational practicality among them – have seen its principles applied in everything from the composition of the first meteorological chart by Edmond Halley in 1686 to the first satellite map of the United States in 1974. Google, along with countless other internet map providers, continues to cleave to Mercator, despite the arrival of alternative mapping schemes developed since 'pin-point-accurate' satellite geolocation became available.

Perhaps deep down this is an admission of sorts that, even in an era when few activities online or out in the real world go untracked, the map can never truly be the territory, as the old adage has it.

We look to maps to lead us where we need to go, just as our ancestors did, but the journey can sometimes be as interesting as the destination, and the chart as delightful as the ground covered. After all, Mercator never set sail on any ocean himself, neither did he appear to have travelled much beyond the Low Countries, but by giving us the world on paper, he created a form in the atlas for imaginative suggestion and dreaming as much as scientific exploration.

The world has become both larger and smaller since Mercator's day, when swathes of it remained subject to rumour, myth and speculation. Our internet-aided present puts the once entirely unknown at our fingertips, distorting distances in time and space beyond anything previously imagined in cartography. Surprises, we are led to believe, are thinner on the ground now, because almost everything can be seen on a screen. Yet the unexpected, a term that dates back to the 1580s and the period when Mercator was perfecting his projection maps, has not been banished entirely. Our appetite for the unusual, the out of the ordinary has, if anything, only been heightened by new technology. The scanning and sharing of fresh information and imagery provides a spur to seeking out fresh destinations and experiences, just as the original Atlas did in its day.

Atlas of the Unexpected, then, is a compendium of places – odd and enchanting, ancient and modern – touched by the certainty of chance and the often haphazard nature of what passed for discovery in the golden age of exploration. Expect the unexpected to come from some element of a site's geography, architecture, or present or past state of being. Unimaginable in some instances, and all but uninhabitable in others, these are places with stories to tell that help remind us of the enduring strangeness of our planet.

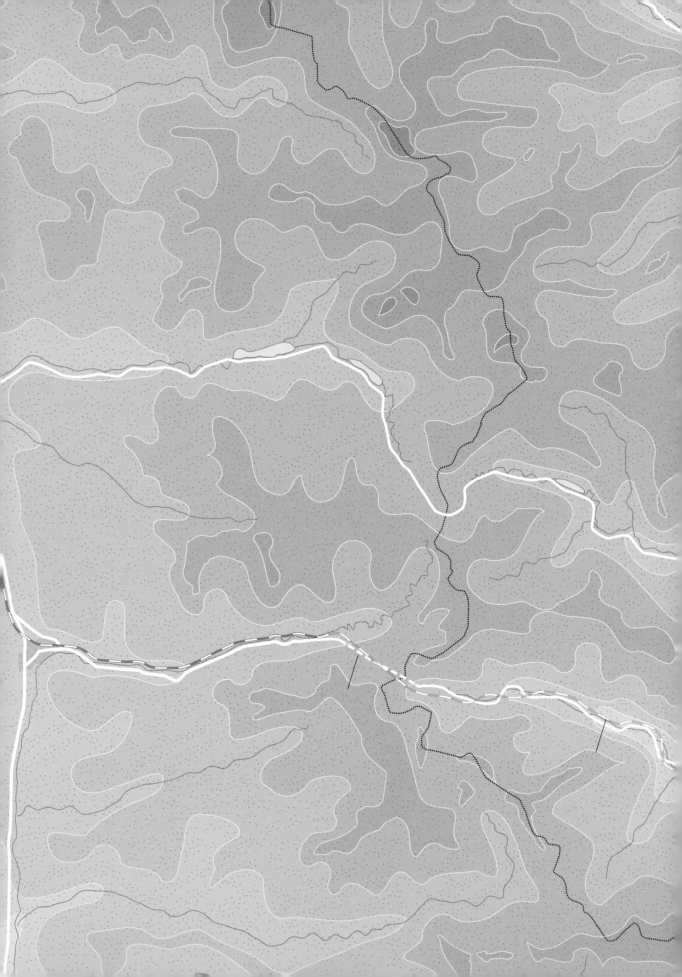

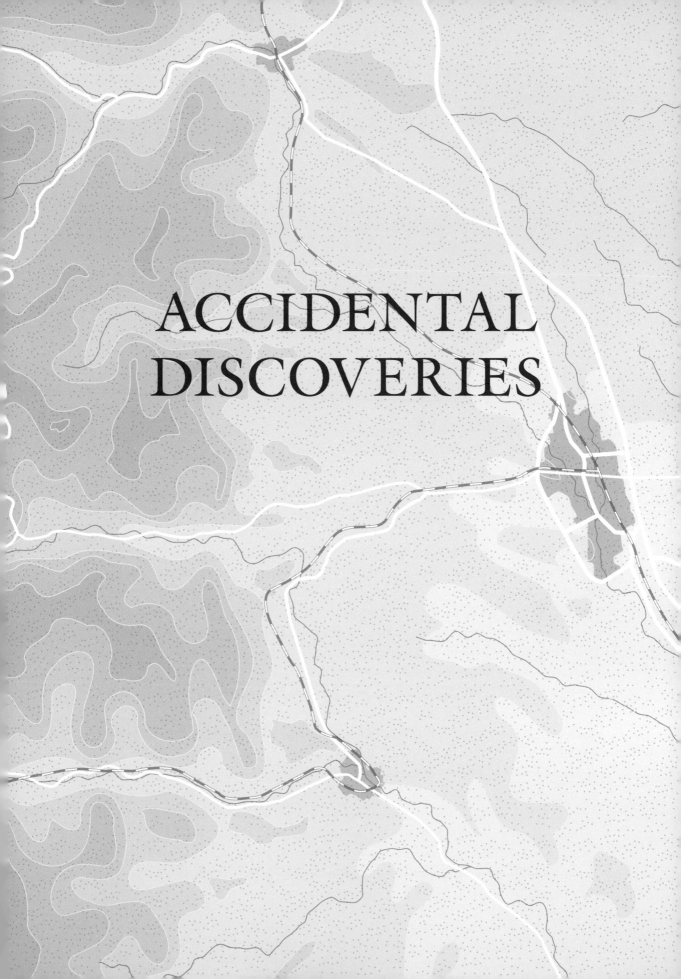

ACCIDENTAL
DISCOVERIES

MADEIRA ARCHIPELAGO

PORTUGAL

Atlantic Ocean

The discovery – or, more accurately, rediscovery – of Madeira and its neighbours Porto Santo and the Desertas Islands, is said to have involved two accidents: one happy and the other not. The less fortunate of the two did at least have what might, in a Hollywood movie, be called 'a love interest'. Something the two 'accidents' have in common with each other – and, in fact, with one of the earliest historical accounts of the Madeiran archipelago – is inclement weather.

That historical account is attributed to the Roman lawyer Pliny the Younger, in his *Natural History* of around AD 77, where he described a band of sailors voyaging for the Fortunate Isles (the Canary Islands) being blown off course in a gale and reaching a distant archipelago in the Atlantic Ocean, known at the time as the Purple Islands. The name referred to the brightly coloured dyes apparently produced there: Madeira is blessed with a rich stock of subtropical dragon trees (*Dracaena draco*), whose deep-red resin continues to find use as a pigment to this day.

The two 'accidental' stories are more colourful than Pliny's account, however, and perhaps the most intriguing begins – at least according to the legend – in England, in 1344, with Robert Machin, a maritime trader of noble-ish blood and a ship, *La Welyfare*. Machin had fallen in love with Ana d'Arfet and she with him. Unfortunately, d'Arfet belonged to one of the most distinguished families in the land, making marriage between the two all but impossible in a feudal society in which rank was policed with unwavering avidity. To escape what have been recorded as 'the persecutions of the damsel's father', the couple decided to elope. Recruiting a skeleton crew for *La Welyfare*, they set sail for the Mediterranean. There, they met with a fierce northeasterly wind, which carried them far out into the Atlantic Ocean. After some thirteen days or more, they arrived at a deserted,

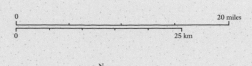

0   20 miles

0   25 km

Porto Santo

VILA BALEIRA

Cal Islet

N

A T L A N T I C   O C E A N

PORTO MONIZ

PONTA
DELGADA

SAO JORGE

FAIAL

Pico Ruivo

CALHETA

MACHICO

RIBEIRA BRAVA

SANTA CRUZ

FUNCHAL

CANIÇO

M A D E I R A

*Deserta
Grande*

*Desertas
Islands*

Bugio

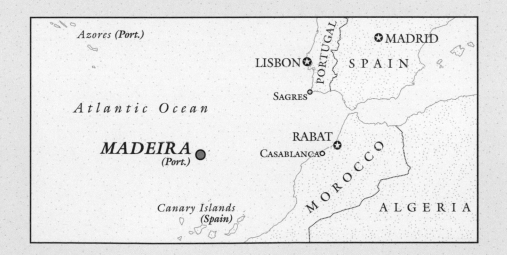

Azores (Port.)

PORTUGAL

✪ MADRID

LISBON ✪

SPAIN

Atlantic Ocean

Sagres ⊙

MADEIRA
(Port.) ●

RABAT ✪

Casablanca ⊙

MOROCCO

*Canary Islands
(Spain)*

ALGERIA

unknown island, whose jagged, volcanic terrain was covered with emerald-green vegetation and forests of laurel trees. Such pleasing verdure was not to stop the blue-blooded Ana dying almost immediately of exposure; heartbroken, her lover followed her a week or so later. After burying the couple, the crew opted to quit the island, only then to be picked off by Moroccan pirates and imprisoned or sold into slavery at Fez. Today, accounts of how this tale reached the world at large vary. In most versions, however, the events are relayed to one Juan de Morales, a Spanish marine pilot famed for his navigational skills who, by chance, happened to be in the same Moroccan gaol as a couple of Machin's unfortunate mariners. From Morales, via one means or another (ransom payments, kidnap, shipwreck among them) – and with some discrepancies as to the dates – the story of the island and the ill-starred lovers reached the Portuguese court of Prince Henry the Navigator. At the time, the royal prince, one of the greatest advocates of maritime exploration of his age, was busy despatching ships to the Barbary Coast, which marks the beginning of the second 'accidental' discovery of Madeira.

In 1418, a vessel under the command of João Gonçalves Zarco and Tristão Vaz Teixeira was, at Henry's behest, tracking the coast of Guinea when it, too, was battered by a fearsome storm and cast upon an unknown island. The landmass was immediately

christened Porto Santo (Holy Harbour), the sailors praising a merciful God who had not cast them onto the rocks or sent them over the edge of the known world. The only thing visible beyond this small island was an ominous-looking dense, dark cloud to the southwest. Saner heads on the boat wondered if this might not be another island covered in mist. The majority, on the other hand, were certain these were 'vapours rising from the mouth of hell'; to venture any further was to risk dropping off the edge of the world and falling into a bottomless pit where only fiendish serpents and monsters awaited. Zarco and Teixeira therefore returned to Sagres, in the Algarve, to report what they had found.

Having less truck with the accepted topography of the world, Henry sent Zarco, Teixeira and the Genoese navigator Bartolomeu Perestrelo, and a flotilla of three ships, to settle Porto Santo for Portugal. He also ordered them to conduct an expedition to investigate the strange cloud. In July 1420, without the aid of storms or the intervention of serpents, Zarco and Teixeira finally reached a thickly forested island that they named Madeira – or the Island of Wood – in honour of its trees.

BELOW: Madeira's islands are the summits of once-volcanic mountains that rise from the floor of the Atlantic Ocean.

DERINKUYU UNDERGROUND CITY

TURKEY

Cappadocia

One of the best-loved and longest-standing establishments in London's East End is a Turkish restaurant called the Stone Cave. True to its name, stepping into this eatery, which is housed in a pretty standard nineteenth-century terrace, is like entering a giant cave. The walls bulge out into the room with fake rock panels and the ceiling is a canopy of ersatz stalactites crafted from some ingenious material. The food and service are both excellent and affordable, and the ambience never less than convivial. Once there, sitting on a comfortably cushioned bench with a dish of hummus and a basket of warm flatbread on the table in front of you, the aromas of garlic and toasted sesame seeds in the air, the notion of eating inside a cave couldn't seem more natural. Yet the idea of a cave as a habitat is something we have been moving away from since the Stone Age. We even use the terms 'cave dweller' and 'troglodyte' as pejoratives; they are synonymous with the brutal and the primitive. In ancient mythology and fairy stories, ogres and dragons live in caves. As hideaways, of course, they have their advantages, as the superhero Batman and more than a few Bond villains have shown. This fact was also not lost on the inhabitants of Derinkuyu in Cappadocia, an area of Turkey in central Anatolia, in Byzantine times.

In AD 364, Emperor Valentinian I divided the Roman empire into western and eastern sections, giving rule of the latter to his brother, Valens. Cappadocia, a Roman province for the previous three hundred years, came under the jurisdiction of the Eastern Roman Empire with Constantinople as its capital. This Roman city had been erected by the first Christian emperor, Constantine I, on the site of the ancient Greek colony of Byzantium, some thirty years earlier. Under constant attack from marauding Germanic invaders such as the Visigoths, the Western Roman Empire gradually crumbled away, falling entirely in AD 476, when the barbarian Flavius Odoacer sacked Rome and overthrew the last Roman emperor,

Romulus Augustus. Although Rome was finished, the eastern, Byzantine, half of the empire survived and continued to thrive for another one thousand years.

The Byzantine empire experienced long periods of military and political power, as well as wealth and stability, where trade and the arts and culture flourished. At its peak in the fifth century, the empire commanded territories in North Africa, Asia Minor and much of Mediterranean Europe. The empire also faced incursions from Muslim Arabs and the Seljuk Turks from Central Asia who, having conquered Persia, pushed into Cappadocia and took Anatolia in 1071. Prior to this, the region served as the last outpost of the Byzantine empire, a Christian enclave before Muslim Syria, with the Taurus mountains to the east forming a natural frontier between them. As such, the region was no stranger to raids and towns like Derinkuyu took some rather elaborate measures to defend themselves.

Just how elaborate these measures were was not fully understood until 1963, however. It was in this year that one Derinkuyu man, embarking on some improvements to his property, knocked a wall out in his basement. The removal of the wall revealed a passageway that led down into a vast network of secret underground tunnels, staircases and chambers. Equipped with ventilation shafts and a well, this subterranean lair could have accommodated more than 20,000 people. It was kitted out for long stays, with storerooms, kitchens, dining rooms, cellars, chapels and, quite possibly, a school. Each floor was sealed with a hefty stone door that could be locked from the inside to prevent unwanted intruders from entering the network at any level.

It is believed that the earliest sections of this hidden metropolis could well have been carved out by the ancient Phrygians, who ruled Anatolia back in the seventh century BC, but whatever bunkers and tunnels the Phrygians established beneath Derinkuyu, it is generally agreed that significant expansion occurred in Byzantine times – an epoch when the area's inhabitants had reason enough to feel beleaguered and in need of a protective bolthole. Wilder theories about the age, origins, construction and intended use of these underground rooms abound. Whatever their roots – and they were seemingly only abandoned in the opening decade of the twentieth century – the caves have, since their rediscovery, become a popular visitor attraction, with guided tours conducted for a fee.

RIGHT: Deep underground at Derinkuyu. Today, the complex runs to some eleven floors, although there may still be more, deeper down, that is yet to be excavated.

41° 34' 37.2" N 79° 38' 54.8" W

VASELINE
USA

Titusville, Pennsylvania

Titusville, Pennsylvania, is probably not on many people's maps these days. Most Americans, if questioned, might fail even to recognise the name. Yet, for a time, the city blazed as brightly as any place in the United States – if not the world. Just as Hollywood is synonymous with movies, and the Klondike with gold, Washington with government and Maryland with crabs, Titusville was once famous for one single thing. That single thing, before Texas or Qatar, was oil.

There had, of course, long been oil in this part of Pennsylvania; there had also been beech, birch, sugar maple, white pine and oak trees – at one time so dense that the region was predominantly forest. But it was not the presence of oil in the creeks, or seeping here and there out of the ground, that had attracted the town's founder to the area in 1790. That man, one Jonathan Titus, was a civil engineer who had conducted surveys for the Holland Land Company and, for him, the region's prospects lay in its topography: a 5-km-long (3-mile) valley sandwiched between two hills, where a farm might comfortably nestle.

Oil, for the majority of the town's earliest pioneers, was more of a nuisance than anything else, since it spoiled saltwater wells and soil that might otherwise have been turned over to cultivation. This situation had changed by the 1850s, however, when such oil deposits came to be considered as a potential substitute for the rapidly depleting global supplies of whale oil and the new, if too costly for most, coal gas. Both were used extensively for lighting lamps, in preference to tallow or wax candles.

In 1858, Edwin Drake was an unemployed railroad conductor in his forties, who had been invalided by illness resulting from his former profession. The Seneca Oil Company hired Drake and dispatched him to Titusville, to investigate deposits of oil in land belonging to the company's investors. A year later, Drake perfected a means of boring

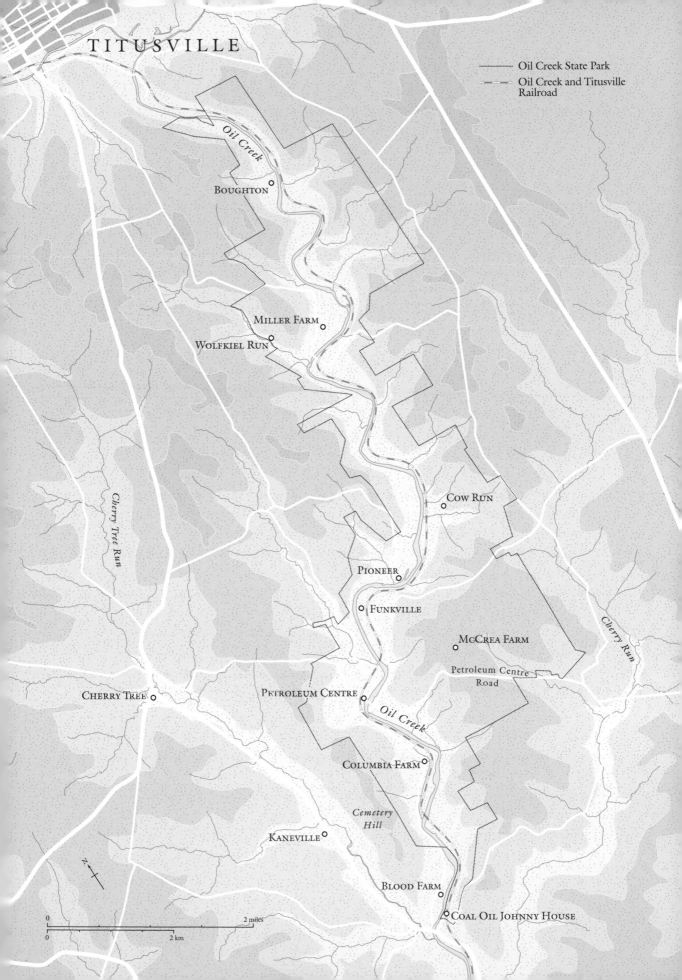

TITUSVILLE

Oil Creek

BOUGHTON

MILLER FARM
WOLFKIEL RUN

Cherry Tree Run

COW RUN

PIONEER

FUNKVILLE

McCREA FARM

Petroleum Centre
Road

Cherry Run

CHERRY TREE

PETROLEUM CENTRE

Oil Creek

COLUMBIA FARM

Cemetery
Hill

KANEVILLE

BLOOD FARM

COAL OIL JOHNNY HOUSE

.... Oil Creek State Park
— — — Oil Creek and Titusville
Railroad

N

0   2 miles
0   2 km

for oil using a metal pipe that pumped it out of the ground and into barrels. Virtually overnight, Titusville became a boomtown – oil derricks were said to have gone up so fast and so thick that 'they blotted out the trees'. No mean feat in a district famed, until only comparatively recently, for its lumber mills.

Sadly, Drake himself, a poor businessman too fond of river fishing to pay adequate attention to his fiscal arrangements, failed utterly to profit from oil. He spent his final years in sickness and subsisting on a small pension doled out by the state of Pennsylvania – a rather meagre thank you for his contribution to the birth of industry in the area. Meanwhile, vast sums were to be made, attracting many prospectors to Titusville. One such man was the twenty-two-year-old, English-born New Yorker, Robert Chesebrough. As a chemist with a background in converting the soon-to-be-obsolete whale oil into kerosene, he had supposedly spent his life savings on the trip, and was perhaps keener than most new arrivals to make good on that investment.

Strangely, Chesebrough's curiosity was piqued not by the oil itself – by the time of his arrival in Titusville that was in the hands of a select few. No, instead, Chesebrough became fascinated by an odd, and almost wholly ill-regarded gunk that emerged from the pumping process. Known as 'rod wax' by the oil riggers, this dark, viscous sludge came up with the crude oil and, if not scraped off, caused the machinery to clog up entirely. So far, so unappealing. But some of the oilmen alluded to some special medicinal quality of the substance, reporting that it did help heal cuts and bruises they sustained on the job.

Similar claims had once been made of Titusville's oil itself, which had first been marketed as a tonic. One Sam Kier, an enterprising local canal-boat operator, had, for instance, sold fifty-cent bottles of crude as Kier's Rock Oil, 'Nature's Remedy, from Four Hundred Feet Below the Earth's Surface'. But the commodity was now far too valuable as an illuminant to be wasted on the sick and elderly of Philadelphia. Rod wax, on the other hand, as Chesebrough cannily noted, was going spare.

Refining the wax into a clear, odourless substance, Chesebrough obtained the patent for his particular 'snake oil' in 1872. He dubbed it 'Vaseline', from the German for water and the Greek for oil. Having spent some time testing it on himself, he began peddling it as a curative for grazes, burns and wounds. In classic medicine-show mode, he took to the road and gave demonstrations in which he purposely stabbed and seared himself, before applying his miraculous salve. Slowly, but surely, Vaseline caught on and is still with us today – its name far more familiar around the world than that of Titusville, Pennsylvania. Chesebrough lived to ninety-six and in his dotage attributed his longevity to having eaten a spoonful of the stuff every day for years. Contemporary science discounts the idea that Vaseline is any special kind of wonder drug, but as a so-called 'occlusive moisturiser', it does help keep moisture in and dirt and bacteria out of minor abrasions, making it an effective enough remedy for chapped lips and nappy rash.

ABOVE: While prospectors in Titusville were busy pumping for lucrative oil, Robert Augustus Chesebrough was more interested in the greasy sludge that threatened to clog their machinery.

31° 44' 28.2" N 35° 27' 32.8" E

THE DEAD SEA SCROLLS

ISRAEL

Qumran

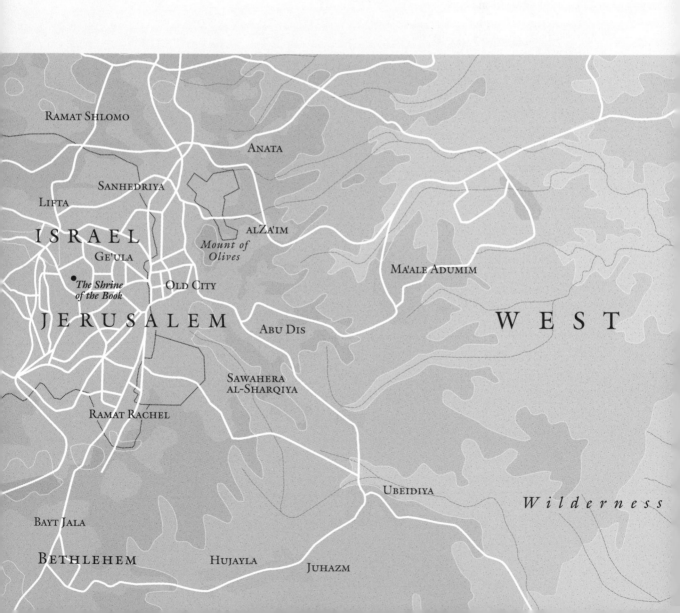

RAMAT SHLOMO

ANATA

SANHEDRIYA

LIFTA

ISRAEL

GE'ULA

alZa'im

Mount of Olives

MA'ALE ADUMIM

•*The Shrine of the Book*

OLD CITY

JERUSALEM

WEST

ABU DIS

SAWAHERA AL-SHARQIYA

RAMAT RACHEL

UBEIDIYA

Wilderness

BAYT JALA

BETHLEHEM

HUJAYLA

JUHAZM

Goats tend to get something of a raw deal in the Bible. In the Old Testament books of Leviticus and Numbers, God demands that they be offered up as sacrifices to atone for a variety of sins. Worse still, perhaps, is the New Testament gospel of Matthew, which contains a parable about Judgement Day, when Jesus will return to Earth to set about dividing the blessed from the cursed. The former are equated with sheep and promised possession of 'the kingdom which has been prepared for you ever since the creation of the world'. The latter are compared to goats, and are to be dispatched to 'the eternal fire which has been prepared for the Devil and his angels!' The choice of animals is far from arbitrary. Implicit is the idea that sheep, docile creatures with strong herding instincts, are, like true believers, to be rewarded for their loyalty and that goats, more truculent and independent, are, as with those who refuse to heed the word of God, to be punished for their wilfulness. Yet it is a stray goat that we have to thank for one of the most important finds of Biblical material ever made: the discovery of the Dead Sea Scrolls.

Qumran is about 1.6 km (1 mile) northwest of the Dead Sea, a salt lake that lies below sea level in a region commonly referred to as 'the Wilderness of Judea'. A rocky hill of desert crevasses leavened by a few patches of waving, sunburnt yellow grass, the area has one

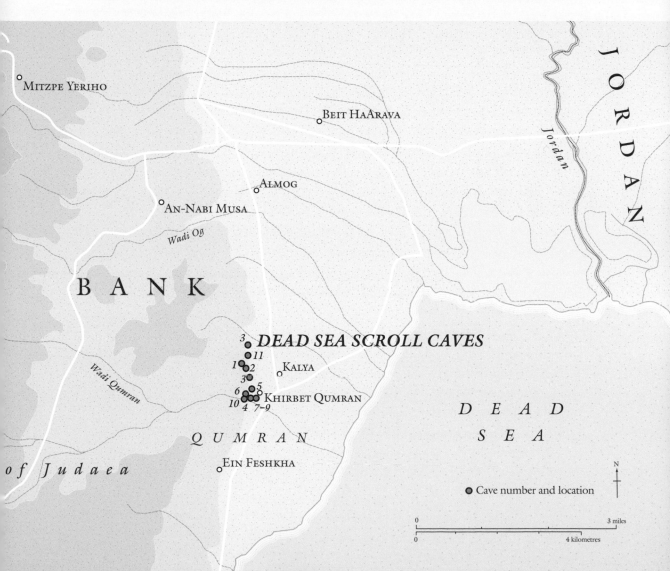

freshwater spring, Ein Feshkha. Around 100–125 BC, the bleakness of the area attracted a devoutly religious Jewish sect, who settled here until seemingly disrupted by an earthquake in around 31 BC. Subsequent inhabitants were removed in AD 68, when troops of Roman Emperor Vespasian swept through and briefly claimed part of the site for a military base. The region remained largely uninhabited from this time onwards.

In the early summer of 1947, a few goatherds of the Ta'amireh people were leading their flock through this barren range on their way from Jordan to Bethlehem. It became apparent that one of the goats had gone missing and so the shepherd boy, Muhammed 'ed-Dib' (nick-named the Wolf) Ahmed el-Hamid, was dispatched to look for it. In time he came across the entrance to an underground cavern. It was little more than a crack but just large enough for a goat to fall through. The boy tossed a stone down into the opening hoping to discover whether the kid was trapped below. Instead of hearing a startled bleat or simply rock glancing off rock, the boy heard the distinct sound of pottery shattering. Peering down into the cave, he could just make out what looked like a number of large earthenware jars. Convinced that these jars must contain something valuable, the boy persuaded another of his tribesmen to return the following day. What they found inside the jars was not gold and jewels, but a handful of scrolls made from ancient animal parchment and covered in an esoteric script that no one could decipher.

Through a member of the Syrian community, the scrolls and their discoverers found themselves at the door of Athanasius Yeshue Samuel, the metropolitan (or archbishop) of the Syrian Orthodox archdiocese of Jerusalem. Samuel was known to be an avid collector of material in Syriac, the ancient variant of the Aramaic language in which many early Christian texts were written. On inspection, however, the language on the scrolls was not Syriac, but ancient Hebrew, which Samuel could not read. Acting on a hunch, the metropolitan bought four of the scrolls for a reported fee of $250. (Three more scrolls from the same cave, went to a buyer at the Hebrew University in Jerusalem.)

Gradually the texts were identified as, perhaps, the earliest extant, complete copy of the book of Isaiah, a commentary upon the Jewish prophet Habakkuk, and a manual of ancient rituals, rules and discipline. Further study was interrupted by the outbreak of the Arab–Israeli War in 1948. Initially the scrolls were held in the Beirut bank vault for their protection, but later rejoined Samuel who had emigrated to America for safety. On 1 June 1954, Samuel put the scrolls up for sale with an advert in *The Wall Street Journal* that ran: 'Biblical manuscripts dating back to at least 200 BC for sale. This would be an ideal gift to an educational or religious institution by an individual or group.' This time, the closing price was $250,000 and their buyer a Mr Sydney Estridge, an American businessman covertly acting as a middleman for the state of Israel.

The scrolls returned to Jerusalem to be reunited with the other three scrolls, and where they were joined by arcane parchments retrieved from later excavations in the area. In due course all were housed in a new purpose-built museum called The Shrine of the Book, which remains open today. Whatever became of the goat, meanwhile, is alas, undocumented.

BELOW: The Wilderness of Judea. Over time, significant documents were discovered in eleven caves across the region.

CAHOKIA MOUNDS

USA

Illinois

Movies are all about transportation. They take us to some other place, showing us whole worlds beyond our experience and imagination. In the Golden Age of Hollywood, picture houses themselves were frequently designed to resemble Assyrian palaces or Egyptian monuments. The designs of such buildings were as epic and outlandish as the exotic sword-and-sandal swashbucklers dished up by studio moguls such as Cecil B. DeMille. In 1933, Richard M. Hollingshead Jr, the owner of Whiz Auto Products, a company specialising in vehicle waxes and polishes, succeeded in combing two of twentieth-century America's greatest obsessions, the car and the cinema, when he opened the world's first drive-in movie theatre in Camden, New Jersey.

Offering something akin to a private box in a traditional theatre, in which your car became the space from which you could watch a film under the stars and smoke, eat and drink without disturbing your fellow moviegoers, drive-ins were an immediate hit with young families and courting couples. Their heyday came in the baby-boomer era that followed the Second World War, with attendances in America overtaking those of standard cinemas in 1951. However, it wasn't long before television, VCRs and cable networks brought film into people's living rooms, sending the drive-in into terminal decline.

One such victim of changing American viewing habits was the Falcon Drive-In near Collinsville, outside East St Louis, Illinois, which closed in 1983. Born as the Mounds Drive-In in 1949, it was renamed in 1960 in honour of the popular 'compact' Ford Falcon sedan, a car with a chromium grille that resembled a whale's mouth and a fuel-efficiency admired by all. At the time, of course, the world was largely ignorant of – or, at least, mostly indifferent to – the environmental costs of car use and whole towns and cities were busily being reconfigured to accommodate the rising numbers of finned gas guzzlers. The car was

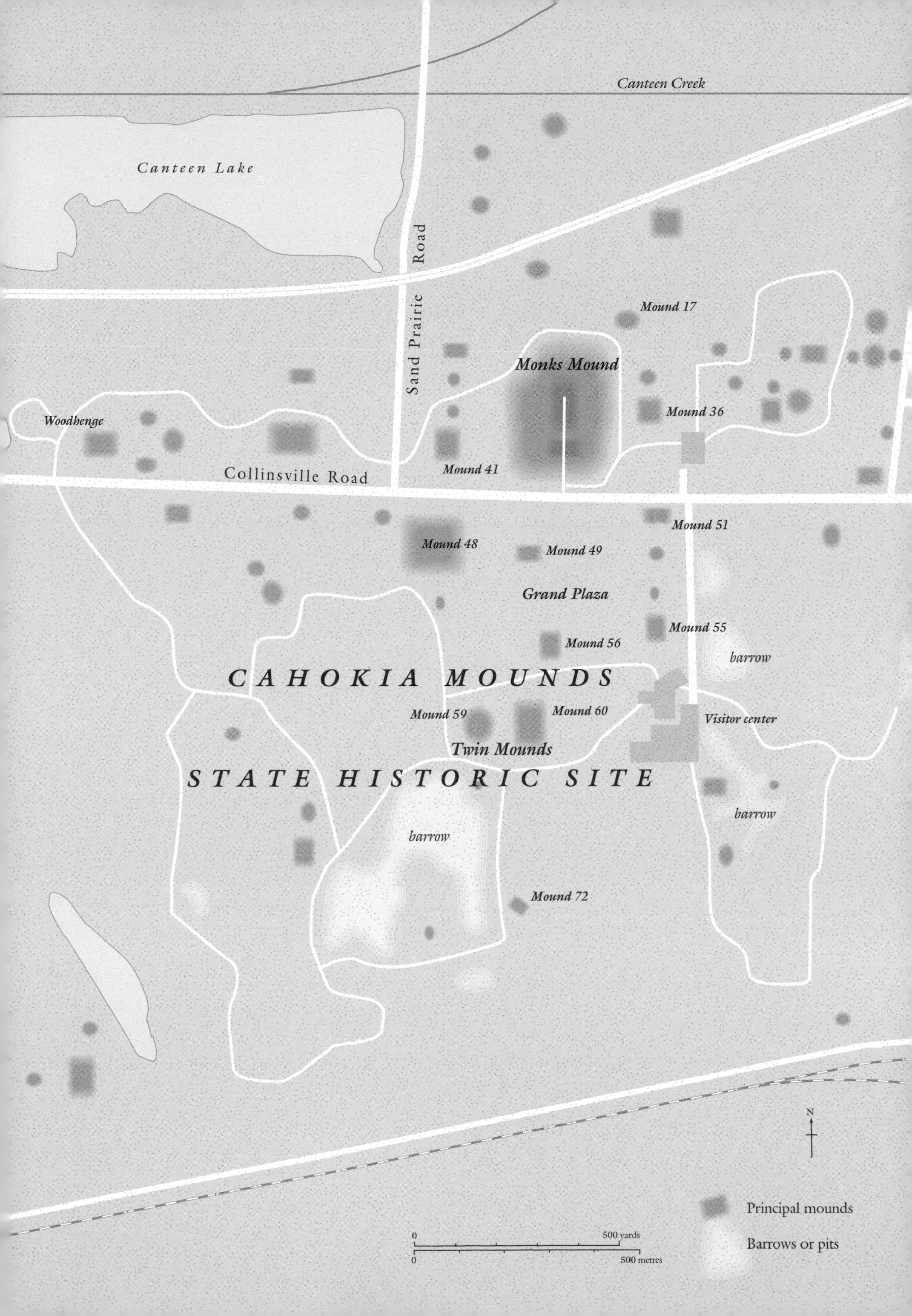

Canteen Creek

Canteen Lake

Sand Prairie Road

Mound 17

Monks Mound

Mound 36

Woodhenge

Collinsville Road

Mound 41

Mound 51

Mound 48

Mound 49

Grand Plaza

Mound 55

barrow

Mound 56

CAHOKIA MOUNDS

Mound 59

Mound 60

Visitor center

Twin Mounds

STATE HISTORIC SITE

barrow

barrow

Mound 72

N

0   500 yards

0   500 metres

Principal mounds

Barrows or pits

heralded as an emblem of human progress, and no one, it was argued, should stand in its way. Nothing perhaps exemplifies this attitude more than the creation of this particular Illinois drive-in. Few of those pulling up in their Plymouth Belvederes or Chevrolet Impalas would have given much thought to the mounds that had given the area its original name. Nor would they have been especially bothered to learn that some of those mounds had been levelled by bulldozers to make room for the very facility that allowed them to relax in comfort on their bench seats while *The Blob*, say, flickered on the big screen in front of them. Yet beyond the perimeter of that drive-in, and deep beneath the tread of their whitewall tyres, were the last remaining fragments of an ancient American metropolis that had once extended over 15.5 km² (6 sq miles).

That city – Cahokia – was probably the most magnificent American city north of Mexico at its peak, and is believed to have been built by the Mississippians. Centuries before the first European Spanish explorer Hernando de Soto reached these parts in 1540, this little-known Native American tribe dominated the southeastern corner of the continent from the Mississippi River to the shores of the Atlantic Ocean. Farmers, artisans and traders rather than hunter-gatherers, the Mississippians were a sophisticated people far removed from stereotypical Hollywood western portrayals – a drive-in staple for decades.

Cahokia was seemingly a place of religious pilgrimage. Planned along astronomical lines, the city was laid out with a precision and symmetry not dissimilar to that of a postwar suburb like Levittown, Pennsylvania or Chicago's Park Forest, with 120 man-made earthen mounds arranged in rows, and a sequence of terraces and open plazas. At its heart stood a giant mound, 100 feet high and covering 14 acres. Known as the Monk's Mound, after the French Trappist monks who tilled the land here in the opening years of the nineteenth century, it survives today and is the largest prehistoric earthen mound in North America.

With a population of some 10,000 to 20,000 by AD 1050, it remains a mystery why the city was all but abandoned three hundred years later. No adequate theory has been proposed to explain the reason for such a rapid and complete departure by the Mississippians. In the four centuries that followed, nearly one-third of these were lost, ploughed up for farmland and built on. It wasn't until the 1960s that archaeologists began to take a serious interest in Cahokia. Their efforts led to the site being declared a Unesco World Heritage Site in 1982. In the following year the old Falcon drive-in was swept away and its grounds landscaped into Cahokia Mounds State Historic Site. Its name lives on, however, in a nearby picnic area, while the old speaker posts have been recycled as trail markers.

RIGHT: Monk's Mound at Cahokia. Of 120 original mounds, 72 stand today. It is thought that some served as platforms for the city's most important buildings, while others were used as burial chambers.

40° 44' 57.2" N 14° 29' 05.9" E

POMPEII

ITALY

Naples

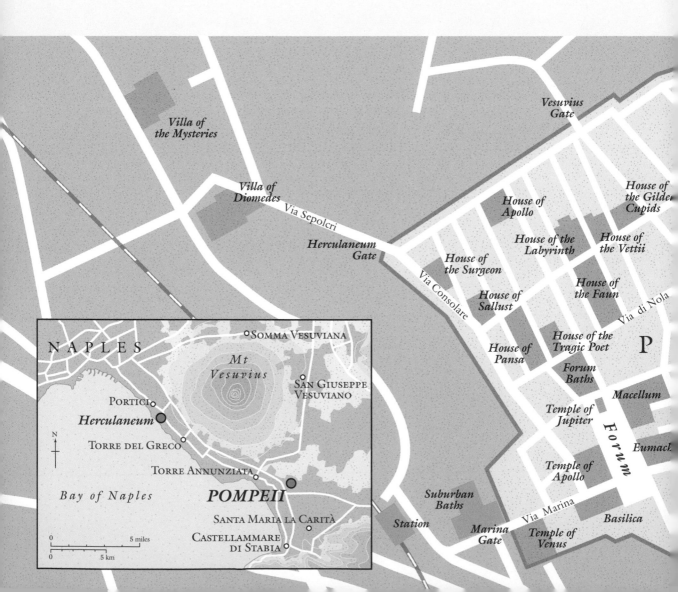

Villa of
the Mysteries

Vesuvius
Gate

Villa of
Diomedes

Via Sepolcri

House of
Apollo

House of
the Gilde
Cupids

Herculaneum
Gate

Via Consolare

House of
the Surgeon

House of the
Labyrinth

House of
the Vettii

House of
Sallust

House of
the Faun

Via di Nola

NAPLES

SOMMA VESUVIANA

House of
Pansa

House of the
Tragic Poet

P

Mt
Vesuvius

SAN GIUSEPPE
VESUVIANO

Forum
Baths

Macellum

PORTICI

Herculaneum

Temple of
Jupiter

F
o
r
u
m

Temple of
Apollo

Eumac

TORRE DEL GRECO

TORRE ANNUNZIATA

POMPEII

Bay of Naples

SANTA MARIA LA CARITÀ

CASTELLAMMARE
DI STABIA

N

Station

Suburban
Baths

Temple of
Venus

Via Marina

Marina
Gate

Basilica

0   5 miles
0   5 km

Starting in triumph and ending in appalling tragedy, Pompeii has been called 'the most found' of all lost cities. But equally it was once one of the most lost – a loss that has since become the sine qua non of its rediscovery and subsequent renown. When Mount Vesuvius erupted on 24 August AD 79, spewing forth molten lava, ash, sulphurous rock and poisonous gas for two solid days, it buried Pompei and its near neighbour Herculaneum under 6 m (19½ ft) of volcanic material. Taken completely by surprise, thousands were incinerated or suffocated in their own homes or died while attempting to flee the disaster.

A senate committee convened by Emperor Titus sought to help survivors and assess the damage with a view to reconstruction. They concluded almost instantly, however, that Pompeii was beyond any hope of rebuilding. Abandoned and soon put out of mind, the city simply became waste ground that, by the Middle Ages, was known only as Civita – roughly, 'dead town' or 'place inhabited in ancient times'. Erased from landscape and memory, the city's name lingered on solely in the back pages of classical history, appearing in Tacitus and Seneca, and in letters by Pliny, whose uncle, Pliny the Elder, perished in the calamity while attempting to mount a rescue mission. No one was looking for Pompeii because no one had any idea it was there in the first place; neither did they particularly care.

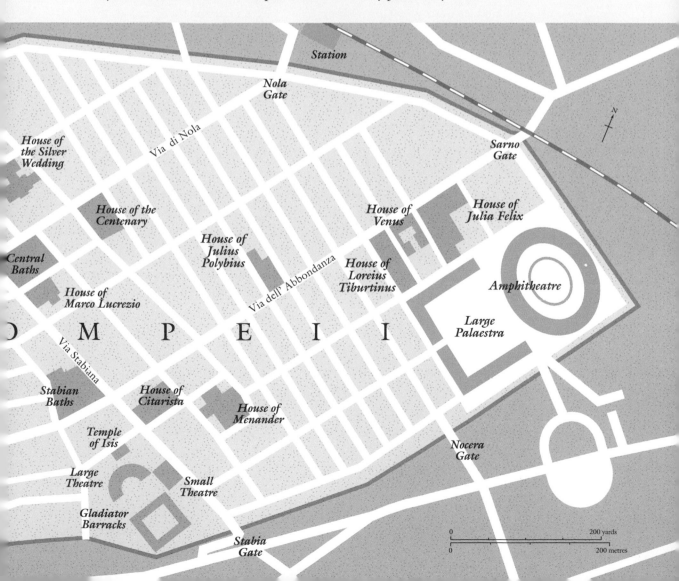

Since it is hard to disentangle the city from its fiery demise, it's worth considering exactly what was lost. According to myth, Pompeii, on the road from Naples to Nocera, was founded by Hercules on his triumphal return from Iberia (Spain), where he'd successfully defeated the monstrous Geryon, making off with the three-bodied giant's prize cattle. These animals formed part of an epic victory parade or *pompa* that happened to wing past Mount Vesuvius. Archaeological evidence points to a settlement here at least as long ago as 600 BC, and with good reason. Looking out across the Mediterranean, and with the limpid waters of the Sarno River to its eastern side, Pompeii arose on a lava spur below Vesuvius, with the black sands of the shore and the salt marshes of the estuary close by. With easy access to the sea, an abundance of fish, fresh water to irrigate crops, and salt for quarrying (the principle ingredient in garum, the fish sauce exported across the empire), the city couldn't help but prosper. The local soil was fertile too, supporting market gardens lined with onions, broad beans, peas and broccoli. Further up the slopes of Vesuvius were vineyards and pine groves. Pompeiians duly gave thanks for their bounty in temples devoted to Jupiter and Apollo, politicked in the Forum, gossiped in city squares, sought entertainment in tavernas, theatres and the *lupanar* (brothels), and cheered on gladiatorial contests in an amphitheatre that, today, is the world's oldest extant example. Seismic tremors were a familiar phenomenon in the area, and an earthquake that shook the city in AD 63 caused such damage that parts of Pompeii were still under repair when Vesuvius blew. Yet the city's citizens seemingly had little inkling that Vesuvius might be volcanic.

Fire and brimstone may have obliterated Pompeii, but water – specifically that of the Sarno River – led to its eventual rediscovery. In the late 1590s, while building a canal through the region, to divert some of the Sarno flow towards Naples, labourers working under the architect Domenico Fontana came across the first few remains of the city while digging out a channel. Failing to see any significance in the charred fragments of stone they'd unearthed, they didn't delve any further. The breakthrough wouldn't come until the eighteenth century, with a chance find that was less easy to dismiss: the excavation of a well in the woods at Frati Alcantarini in about 1709 brought to light the whole shell of one of Herculaneum's theatres. For the next thirty years sculptures and marbles were disinterred pretty much at random until, in 1738, King Charles of Bourbon sponsored a formal excavation of the site. In what is believed to be the first systematic archaeological dig ever undertaken, shafts were sunk deep below ground and a series of tunnels dug to explore the city buried below. Objects of interest were ferried to the surface for inspection and cataloguing. A decade later, and excited by fresh discoveries made further south, attention turned to what finally emerged as Pompeii.

Wars aside – Pompeii was bombed by the Allies in the Second World War – excavation has continued ever since. Given the wear and tear from the millions who visit each year, preserving that which is already unearthed forms an equally vital part of the work carried out. One-third of Pompeii remains underground and there, many archaeologists argue, it should stay. For above it all still towers Vesuvius and, classed as 'one of the world's most dangerous volcanoes', there is no telling when it might awake again.

ABOVE: The Temple of Apollo is one of several temples unearthed at Pompeii. So well preserved are the ruins that they offer insights into ancient Roman life that might otherwise have been lost for ever.

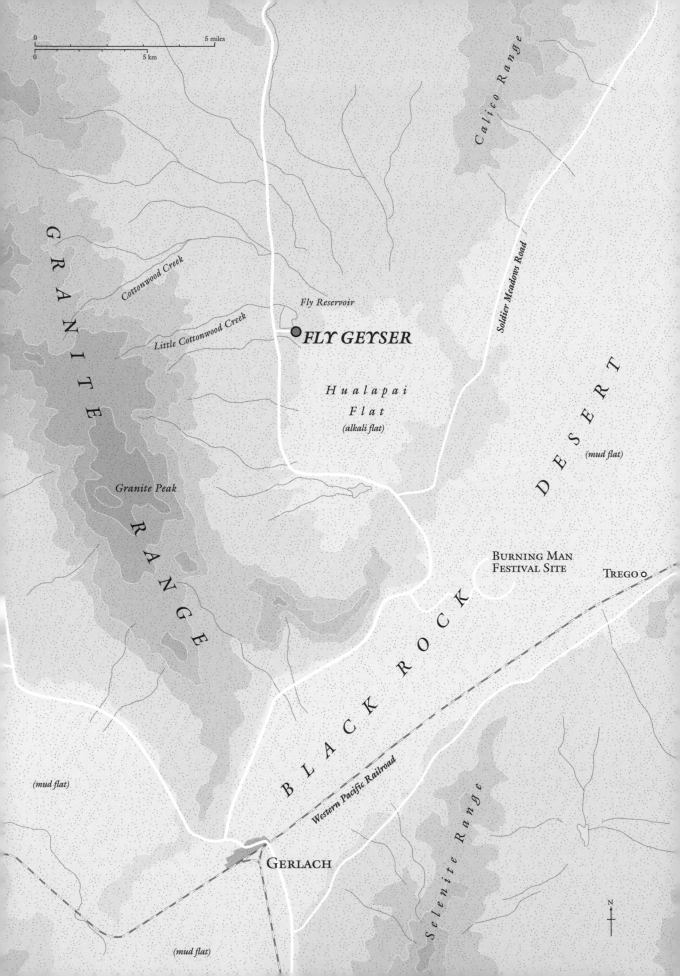

0   5 miles
0   5 km

GRANITE

Cottonwood Creek

Little Cottonwood Creek

Fly Reservoir

● **FLY GEYSER**

*Hualapai
Flat*
(alkali flat)

Calico Range

Soldier Meadows Road

DESERT

(mud flat)

Granite Peak

RANGE

BLACK ROCK

BURNING MAN
FESTIVAL SITE

TREGO ○

(mud flat)

Western Pacific Railroad

Selenite Range

GERLACH

(mud flat)

N

40° 51' 33.6" N 119° 19' 54.8" W

FLY GEYSER
USA
Nevada

The word 'geyser', used to describe a kind of spouting hot-water spring, originates from one single geyser – the Great Geysir in the Haukadalur valley of southern Iceland. Although largely inactive since about 1916, the Great Geysir (*geysir* simply means 'gusher' in Icelandic), could, at one time, be relied upon to spew spectacular jets of scalding water and steam 60 m (200 ft) up into the air nearly every three hours. Awoken by an earthquake in the thirteenth century, the vent's more recent silence has been attributed, in part, to blockage. It is thought that, having been alerted to its existence by sensational newspaper reports and entries in travel guides, the first generation of sightseers in the nineteenth century constantly threw rocks and other junk into its gaping maw. Whatever the truth of that, its near neighbour, Strokkur remains impressively active on a regular and frequent ten-minute basis, albeit with more modest 18-m-high (60 ft) sulphurous jets.

Nevada is a long way from Iceland, both geographically and in terms of flora, fauna and climate. It is the driest state in the United States and predominantly desert or semiarid, while Iceland is described as 'subarctic', although it is milder than its northerly locale might suggest, owing to the warming breezes of the Gulf Steam. However, during the very same year that the Great Geysir decided to give up the ghost, one Nevadan ranch-owner accidentally created a geyser in Washoe County, near the Black Rock Desert. In an attempt to overcome some of the dustiness of his property, the ranchman had begun drilling in the hope of tapping an underground reservoir and establishing a well from which to draw water for irrigation. He definitely hit water, but instead of a cool stream, a fierce torrent of water came bursting out of the ground, geothermically heated and as blazingly hot as the high noon sun. Seeing little value in this steaming monster, the ranchman capped the well and got on with other things. In 1964, however, further drilling work caused the water to burst out again. On this occasion, the gushing water was abandoned and the geyser has spurted on, untamed, ever since. As it happens the water that flows is extremely rich in minerals. Over the decades, the deposits have built up, much in the way that stalagmites do, to leave a curious array of brightly coloured mounds and otherworldly algae-filled pools. The result is a landscape that appears to owe more to science fiction than to the surrounding desert terrain, but one that has grown into an ever-evolving, ecological oasis that sustains a diverse plethora of wildlife.

Since 2016, the property in which the geyser stands has been owned by the organisation that runs the annual Burning Man Festival at nearby Black Rock City. Their stated intention is to turn the site into an eco-arts centre – or, as their website puts it – 'an incubator for the Burning Man community to take ideas from our temporary city and give them a real-world testing ground . . . a place to experiment with shelter, energy, water, environmentalism, new models of living, working and governance.' For the time being, however, the formation is enclosed behind a fence. Nevertheless, several plumes can be seen spouting from the geyser over the top of it and from some miles away.

RIGHT: Fly Geyser stands above pools created
by the calcium carbonate deposits in the
water rising from below the Earth's surface,
at temperatures reaching 200°F (93°C).

GALÁPAGOS ISLANDS

ECUADOR

Pacific Ocean

Several historic accounts of visits to the Galápagos have the ring of disgruntled customer reviews on today's online consumer sites. Herman Melville, the author of *Moby Dick*, passed by in the 1840s while aboard the whaling ship *Acushnet* and in 1854 published *The Encantadas*, a book of sketches of the archipelago, in which he wrote: 'Take five-and-twenty heaps of cinders dumped here and there in an outside city lot, imagine some of them magnified into mountains, and the vacant lot the sea, and you will have a fit idea of the general aspect of the Encantadas, or Enchanted Isles.' It is hardly a flattering description.

Perhaps the archipelago's most famous visitor remains the naturalist, Charles Darwin. Of HMS *Beagle*'s almost five-year-long voyage, Darwin spent a mere five weeks exploring here, setting foot on only four of the main islands. He was evidently excited when, on 7 September 1835, the crew 'steered direct towards the Galápagos Islands . . . [and] novel ground'. It is likely that Darwin had viewed the first scientific specimen of the giant tortoise endemic to Galápagos during a two-year stint he spent studying medicine at the University of Edinburgh. A juvenile example collected by Basil Hall had been preserved in a cask of spirits and donated to the Museum of the College at Edinburgh. His observations of the species on these isolated islands was subsequently to convince him of the possibility of evolution, although years would pass before he presented them in his version of the theory of natural selection in *On the Origin of Species* (1859). It is a popularly held view that the variety in breeds of finches across the Galápagos inspired Darwin's eureka moment; scholars beg to differ, pointing at the paucity of references to the birds in his notes and published writings on evolution before a later, revised edition of *The Voyage of the Beagle* appeared, carrying as it did, sketches of the birds. Darwin recorded as early as 1837, that 'S. American fossils – & species on Galápagos archipelago [are the] origin (especially latter) of all my

views.' Still, this did not stop him from comparing parts of the islands to 'Infernal regions'. Of Albemarle Island he stated: 'I should think it would be difficult to find in the inter-tropical latitudes a piece of land 75 miles long, so entirely useless to man or the larger animals.'

Perhaps the worst review of the Galápagos was the very first. If, quite feasibly, already known to Incan sailors, the islands only came to the attention of Europeans in 1535, and then completely by accident. On 23 February that year, a galleon set sail from Panama carrying Fray Tomás de Berlanga, a local bishop and political bigwig, on a mission to Peru to resolve regional disputes on behalf of King Charles I of Spain. On reaching the equator, the ship encountered a 'six-day-calm'; pulled out into the Pacific by the currents, Berlanga and his crew found themselves in a cartographic no-man's land. It was only on 10 March, with stocks of food and water all but exhausted, that an island, most likely Española, hove into view.

This island failed to supply either fresh water or any edible food. The next island along, probably Floreana, was much larger and looked to offer more, but nothing was immediately forthcoming. The men were so desperate that they tore apart cactuses on the volcanic slopes, sucking out their juices to quench their thirsts. They finally found freshwater in a ravine. Once restored enough to make for the mainland, the Bishop provided a damning parting note, concluding that: 'On the whole island . . . there is no place where one might sow a bushel of corn, because most of it is full of big stones, so much so that it seems as though at one time God had showered stones. What earth there is', he added, 'is like slag, worthless'.

ABOVE: An archipelago of thirteen volcanic islands, the Galápagos straddle the equator in the southeast Pacific Ocean. Most of them have a distinctive conical shape.

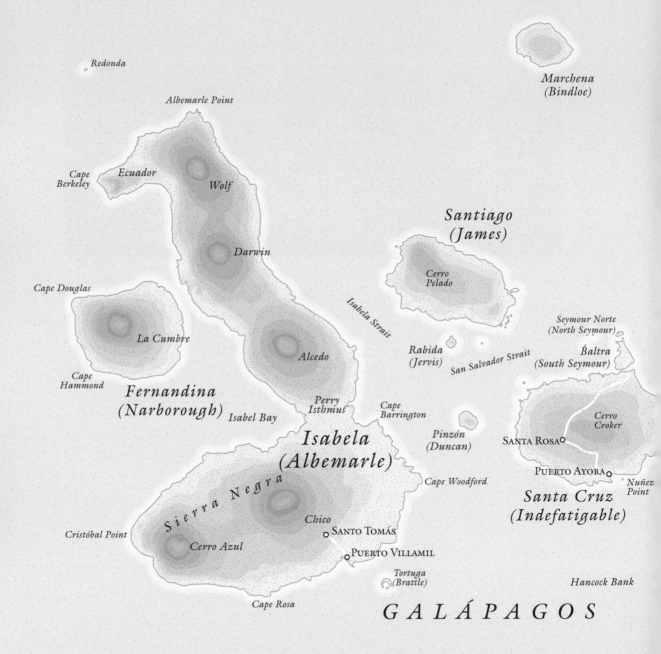

Pinta
(Abingdon)

Marchena
(Bindloe)

Redonda

Albemarle Point

Cape
Berkeley

Ecuador

Wolf

Santiago
(James)

Darwin

Cerro
Pelado

Cape Douglas

Isabela Strait

La Cumbre

Alcedo

Seymour Norte
(North Seymour)

Rabida
(Jervis)

Baltra
(South Seymour)

Cape
Hammond

San Salvador Strait

Fernandina
(Narborough)

Isabel Bay

Perry
Isthmus

Cape
Barrington

Cerro
Croker

Pinzón
(Duncan)

SANTA ROSA

Isabela
(Albemarle)

Cape Woodford

PUERTO AYORA

Nuñez
Point

Sierra Negra

Chico

Santa Cruz
(Indefatigable)

Cristóbal Point

Cerro Azul

SANTO TOMÁS

PUERTO VILLAMIL

Tortuga
(Brattle)

Hancock Bank

Cape Rosa

GALÁPAGOS

Floreana
(Charles)

Gardne

GENOVESA
(Tower)

COSTA RICA
CARTAGENA
PANAMA
VENEZUELA
Pacific Ocean
BOGOTÁ
COLOMBIA
Darwin I.
Wolf I.
GALÁPAGOS
ISLANDS
(Ecuador)
QUITO
ECUADOR
GUAYAQUIL
PERU
BRAZIL

P A C I F I C   O C E A N

Pitt Point

Santa Fé
(Barrington)

PUERTO BAQUERIZO
MORENO

San Cristóbal
(Chatham)

Wreck Point
SAN CRISTOBAL

I S L A N D S

McGowen Reef

N

Suarez Point
Española
(Hood)

0	40 miles
0	50 km

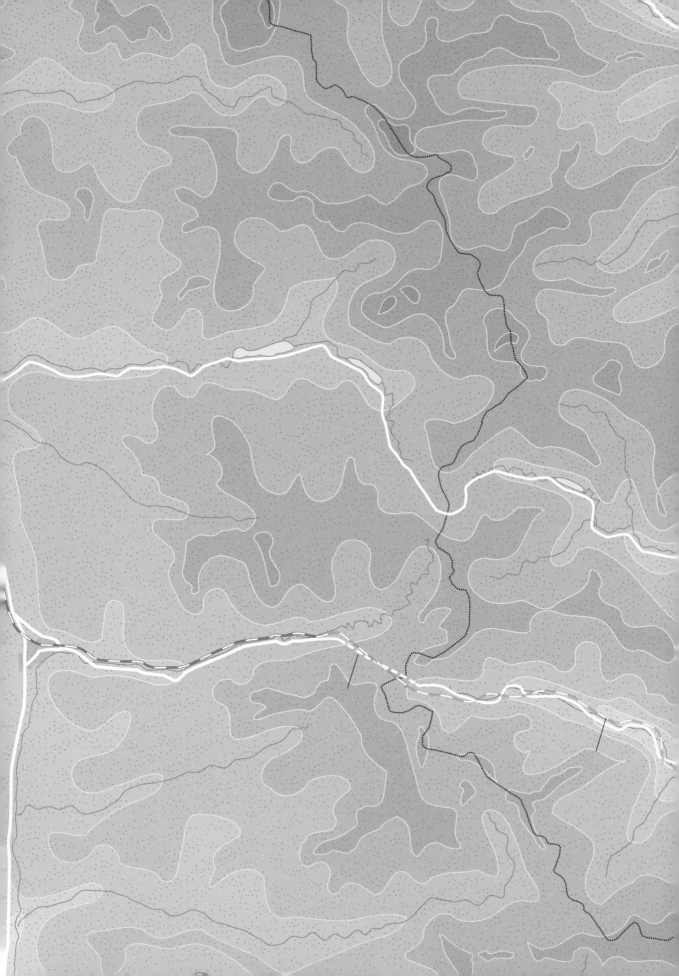

STRANGE
ROOTS

GEORGIA COLONY

USA

Savannah, Georgia

It is the fate of many books to go unread. Thankfully, it is less common for the authors of such works to be punished for the indifference of the reading public. In effect, however, that is what happened to one Robert Castell. In 1728, Castell wrote and self-published, at some expense, *The Villas of the Ancients Illustrated*, a survey of classical Roman architecture, which, at the time, was undergoing a revival among scholars and practitioners of the building arts. Despite this, the book failed to sell in sufficient quantities to cover its printing costs and, unable to pay his creditors, Castell was imprisoned in the Fleet, one of London's most notoriously unsanitary gaols for debtors and bankrupts. Once inside, he fell ill and died in its smallpox-infested sponging house. This abrupt turn of events was especially devastating to James Edward Oglethorpe, a close friend of Castell and one of the few people to have bought, read and admired *The Villas of the Ancients Illustrated*.

Oglethorpe, a solider and member of the landed gentry, held the parliamentary seat of Haslemere and his response to Castell's death was to take up the cause of prison reform. The following year he was appointed to the chair of a House of Commons committee investigating the conditions of the nation's prisons, with a particular focus on the debtor establishments. It was not long before Oglethorpe became frustrated with his new role, seeing the committee's modest suggestions for improvements parried away by vested private interests and public bureaucracy. Just as he began to despair of ever enacting the sort of radical reforms he believed necessary on home soil, it occured to Oglethorpe that there was a whole new world across the Atlantic: the New World of the Americas – a land viewed as a blank canvas, where new ideas might be tried and old ones revived. Oglethorpe began to formulate the idea of establishing a model agrarian colony in America, where freed debtors and those dealt a poor hand through little fault of their own could start afresh in a

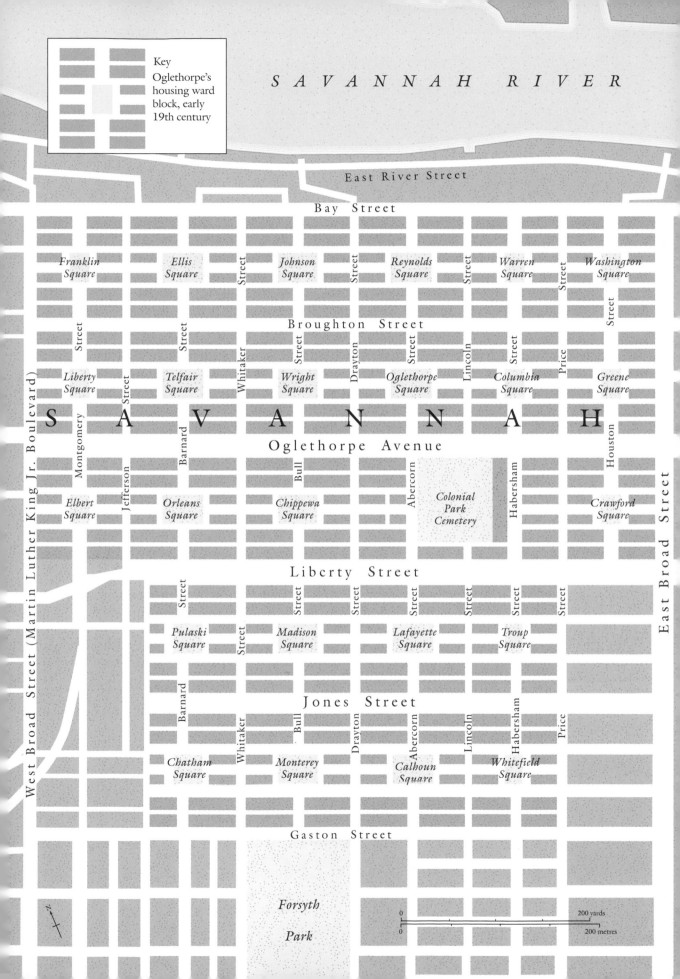

SAVANNAH RIVER

Key
Oglethorpe's housing ward block, early 19th century

East River Street

Bay Street

Franklin Square

Ellis Square

Street

Johnson Square

Street

Reynolds Square

Street

Warren Square

Street

Washington Square

Street

Broughton Street

Street

Street

Whitaker

Street

Drayton

Street

Lincoln

Street

Price

Street

Liberty Square

Street

Telfair Square

Wright Square

Oglethorpe Square

Columbia Square

Greene Square

SAVANNAH

Montgomery

Jefferson

Barnard

Oglethorpe Avenue

Bull

Abercorn

Habersham

Houston

Elbert Square

Orleans Square

Chippewa Square

Colonial Park Cemetery

Crawford Square

West Broad Street (Martin Luther King Jr. Boulevard)

Liberty Street

Street

Street

Street

Street

Street

Street

Street

Pulaski Square

Street

Madison Square

Lafayette Square

Troup Square

East Broad Street

Barnard

Jones Street

Whitaker

Bull

Drayton

Abercorn

Lincoln

Habersham

Price

Chatham Square

Monterey Square

Calhoun Square

Whitefield Square

Gaston Street

Forsyth

Park

0   200 yards

0   200 metres

'place of opportunity for the industrious people of Britain and Europe who have suffered unemployment, poverty, financial misfortune, or religious persecution' under a secular rule of law. Recruiting noted philanthropists, including the Reverend Thomas Bray and Thomas Coram, as backers for the scheme, Oglethorpe successfully petitioned King George II for a grant of land 'southward of Carolina' and the charter for the Georgia Colony, named with a cap doffed to the monarch, was signed in April 1732.

Seven months later, Oglethorpe and 114 colonists sailed for America from Gravesend aboard the frigate *Anne*. Their final destination was a bluff on a bend in the Savannah River, where they set about laying out a town to a preordained plan entirely unprecedented in America. Arguably, its ilk had not been attempted since the days of ancient Rome and the philosopher-builder Vitruvius. For Savannah, Georgia, was to be organised in a series of practical neat grids with twenty-four public squares bypassed by wide transit roads that linked each of six separate wards. Each ward was of equal size and proportion, with the same number of identical house lots. The intention was to erase perceived hierarchies between good and bad neighbourhoods. The underlying order of Oglethorpe's plan hardwired the notion of equality and Enlightenment egalitarianism into the town's core being. Conveying his own commitment to these ideals, Oglethorpe chose to live in a tent while construction took place and would press for the policy of 'equity and beneficence' toward the indigenous Yamacraw people. He also held against the use of slaves in the colony.

Some six thousand colonists settled in Savannah in its first twenty years. Oglethorpe was recalled to England in 1743. Though he never returned to Savannah, he lived long enough to see the colony he'd founded become part of a new independent nation, the United States of America, a country whose Founding Fathers espoused principles not so far removed from his own. Savannah never quite fulfilled its promise as a utopian farming community and springboard for a better society – Oglethorpe lost his battle against the use of slave labour – yet twenty-two of its original squares stand strong and the Oglethorpe plan is esteemed as one of the finest examples of good urban design and to which we are all, ultimately, in the debt of that unfortunate author, Robert Castell.

LEFT: A statue of the colony's founder, James Edward Oglethorpe, stands in Chippewa Square at the heart of the original grid-like development.

CHEMAINUS

CANADA

Vancouver Island

It was lumber that made Chemainus. This small coastal town north of Victoria on the eastern side of Vancouver Island, in the fertile, mountainous Cowichan Valley became wealthy on the back of logging and sawmills. Germans and Scots, and later Chinese and East Indian migrants found work here, beside the Salish Sea. No doubt some of the work was backbreaking and unpleasant, but there were worse places to be – certainly colder ones – for the original First Nation inhabitants titled this valley 'The Warm Land' and the region is noted as one of most temperate in Canada. Today, its claim to the highest national mean annual temperatures and greater hours of sunshine is much trumpeted in contemporary guidebooks. For successive generations that sun had shone on the lumber industry, its rays playing their own part in helping the trees grow through photosynthesis. Every branch of town life was dependent on the spoils of forestry in one way or another. As the price of timber started to wane in the 1970s, however, the business that had defined the place, giving the community its prosperity and a shared sense of purpose, went into free fall. After 120 years in operation, the main sawmill shut down.

Perhaps all that sunshine had naturally predisposed the people of Chemainus to optimism. Where others in similar situations might have given in to despair, the inhabitants here remained determined to see their town survive. Even the town's name derived from that of a native shaman, or spiritual leader, called Tsa-meeunis (Broken Chest), who'd survived a near-mortal wound to lead his people to greatness. Taking succour from this, its elected officials decided to use funds from a government grant to initiate a scheme suggested by Karl Schultz, a local resident of German stock.

On the surface, Schultz's proposal seemed somewhat eccentric, and few were prepared to entertain it at first, but he spent several years seeking support. Since the focus of his

SALISH SEA

VANCOUVER

LANTZVILLE

WELLINGTON

ARBUTUS RIDGE

KERRISDALE

Gabriola
Island

NANAIMO

RICHMOND

SOUTH WELLINGTON

Nanaimo

Valdes Island

Fraser

CASSIDY

DELTA

LADYSMITH

Strait of Georgia

SALTAIR

Galiano
Island

CHEMAINUS

VANCOUVER

CROFTON

Mayne
Island

Chemainus

Salt
Spring
Island

Cowichan
Lake

Cowichan Valley

DUNCAN

North
Pender
Island

Saturna
Island

Cowichan

ISLAND

COWICHAN BAY

CANADA
USA

SWARTZ BAY

SHAWNIGAN LAKE

*Saanich
Inlet*

SIDNEY

San
Juan
Island

BRENTWOOD BAY

San Juan Ridge

CORDOVA BAY

ROYAL OAK

VIEW
ROYAL

LANGFORD

VICTORIA

N

COLWOOD

SOOKE

*Strait of Juan
de Fuca*

0   15 miles
0   20 kms

cause was art and the good of the town, he fortunately found more willing admirers than detractors in the end. What Schultz suggested was that Chemainus should become a living gallery, with a set of large outdoor murals painted on buildings and walls across the town, all depicting different aspects of the area's rich history. These artworks and that heritage, he argued, would attract tourists, bolster civic pride and secure a future for Chemainus as a place in which community, craftsmanship and tradition were championed.

The first five murals were painted in 1982. Their subjects, painted bold and in vivid colours, ranged from a Copper Canyon Railway steam locomotive thundering across the log bridge over the Chemainus River, to the shopfront of the notorious Hong Hing waterfront store and gambling den, operated in the opening decades of the twentieth century by the Chinese entrepreneur Fong Yen Lew. Shutlz's formula worked to perfection and, at the time of writing, Chemainus has more than forty murals and holds an annual mural festival. More profoundly, its example has been copied around the world – most directly, and with similarly impressive effects on the local economy in Sheffield, Tasmania. With over one hundred murals, Sheffield claims to hold world's the largest single collection of public art. Chemainus, however, was the original and the locals naturally claim that it remains the best.

LEFT: Visitors can take a 'mural tour' of the town. Measuring some 31 m (101 ft) in length, *World in Motion* depicts a montage of historic buildings and events between 1883 and 1939 (top). A house in Willow Street bears a portrait of Billy Thomas, a much-loved Chemainus resident (bottom).

42° 44' 09.4" N 25° 23' 37.3" E

BUZLUDZHA MONUMENT

BULGARIA

Stara Zagora Province

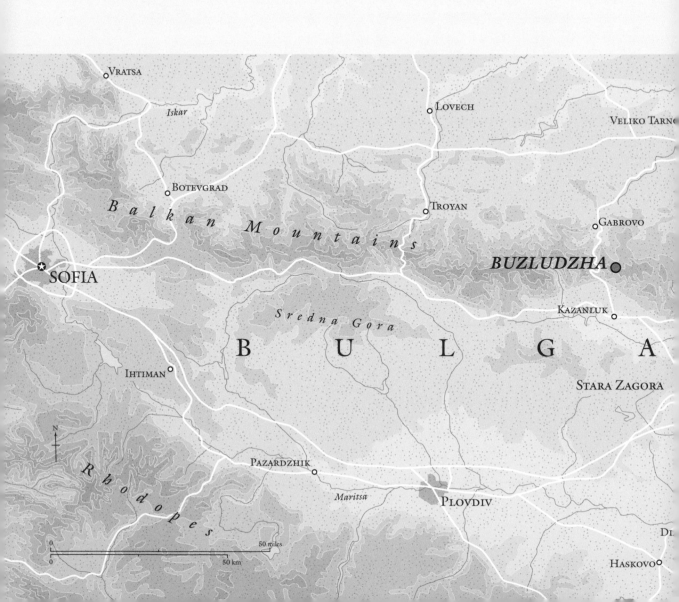

From the Latin *monere* to 'admonish, warn and advise', a monument is, by definition, simply 'something that reminds'. The appearance of the decayed Buzludzha Monument, a graffiti-splattered, concrete, flying-saucer-shaped monolith lodged on a bleak peak of the Balkan Mountains in Bulgaria's central Stara Zagora province, stands as a reminder that not all memories are welcome. This forgotten monument has become a monument to wilful forgetfulness, for mere absent-mindedness could never fully explain its current condition.

Buzludzha Monument Hall was once the most important building in Bulgaria. Its lofty situation ensured it could be seen for miles around – a distinction that holds true today, even if few regard it with quite the same awe and affection as it once engendered. The choice of location, on a brow in the centre of the Shipka Pass, was loaded with significance. It was here, in 1868, that Bulgarian rebels headed by Stefan Karadzha and Hadzhi Dimitar embarked on seemingly hopeless (and in Dmitar's case, fatal) sorties against the might of the Ottoman Empire. The nation's liberation from five hundred years of Turkish rule was finally achieved a decade later during the Russo-Turkish War of 1877–78, when Bulgarian partisans, aided by Russian forces, defeated the Ottomans at Mount Buzludzha in the Battle of Shipka Pass – a victory subsequently memorialised with the erection of a lavishly ornate Muscovite

Orthodox church replete with golden onion domes, that sits swathed in trees and somewhat gaudily incongruence above the rather modest town of Shipka, some 9.5 km (6 miles) to the southwest.

It was on the top of Mount Buzludzha that a band of left-wing radicals convened the first socialist congress in 1891. This gathering resulted in the creation of the Bulgarian Social Democratic Workers' Party (the forerunner of the Bulgarian Communist Party). Given the political history of the location, the choice of meeting place only added to the potency of an occasion marked by high idealism and fiery calls for revolution. The communists came to power in 1946 and, from the late 1950s on, the Bulgarian government held competitions to design appropriate memorials to its forebears to be sited at Mount Buzludzha. Initially the memorials took the form of a trio of statues and engraved reliefs executed in Soviet Realist style. By the 1970s, a new scheme was approved – to build a peak-capping memorial hall and adjacent tower topped by an illuminated red star.

At the suggestion of the building's architect, Georgi Stoilov, its construction was paid for by donations by the Bulgarian people, in a kind of communist prototype of crowdfunding. A large proportion of the 16.2 million levs raised came via the sale of collectable, commemorative stamps. If intended as a celebration of past achievements, Stoilov's design was unashamedly futuristic. Its circular structure, which has distinct hints of Captain Kirk's starship Enterprise from the cult TV show *Star Trek*, required 70,000 tonnes (77,000 tons) of concrete, 3,000 tonnes (3,300 tons) of steel and 40 tonnes (44 tons) of glass. A team of over five hundred soldiers from the construction corps, along with countless artists, engineers, technicians and volunteers, laboured for seven years to complete the building; with temperatures dropping below –30°C (–22°F) in winter here, work was restricted to the milder months between May and September.

The Buzludzha Monument was opened by Todor Zhivkov, General Secretary of the Bulgarian Communist Party on 23 August 1981 – eighty years to the month, if not the day, since the first hillside socialist summit. A likeness of Zhivkov appeared prominently in one of the murals that adorned the walls of the interior of hall, which depicted the history of communism in Bulgaria and generally extolled the virtues of socialism. Pride of place in the centre of the building's domed roof was a gargantuan hammer and sickle. After the fall of the Berlin Wall in 1989 and the subsequent break up the Soviet Union, communist iconography, – no matter how skilfully rendered in multicoloured tiles – became anachronistic. Buzludzha was abandoned to the elements, and then vandalised. Zhivkov was an early casualty, his features chiselled off the wall to leave a blank space behind. That void, like the rest of the Buzludzha Monument, was soon coated with graffiti. For a while the slogan Forget the Past, in English, was daubed in red paint above the wrecked and ravaged entranceway. More recently someone has added the word 'Never' before it. Among international visitors, the growing fame of the Buzludzha Monument as a ruin, and a fresh appreciation of its place in Bulgarian history by a whole generation born since the end of communism, might finally be bringing this long-neglected monument in from the cold.

The monument sits on Buzludzha Peak,
1,432 m (4,698 ft) above the landscape.
Two massive iron fists brandishing flaming
torches stand at the mountain's base.

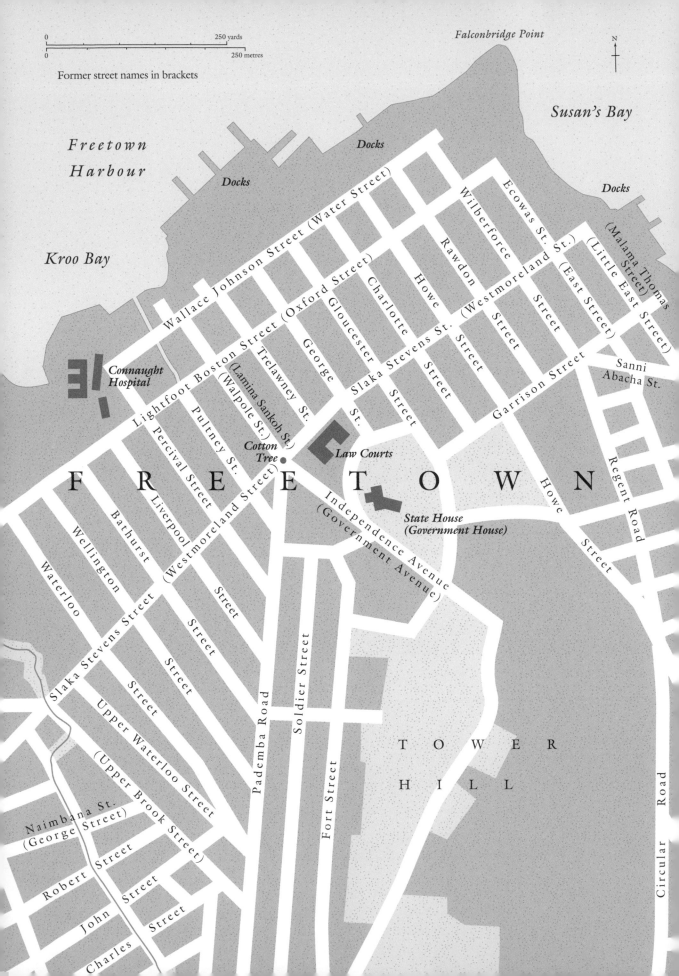

8° 29' 13.4" N 13° 14' 08.1" W

FREETOWN
WEST AFRICA
Sierra Leone

Resting on a peninsula of the Atlantic coast of West Africa, the capital of Sierra Leone is tucked between the verdant mountains and the blue sea. Blessed with one of the world's largest natural harbours, the city is also cursed with the highest annual rainfall in Africa. At the peak of the rainy season in August, some 539.9 mm (21 in) fall on Freetown. Each year flooding is a serious issue and in the summer of 2017 flash floods caused a chunk of Mount Sugar Loaf above the mountainside village of Regent to cave in. Tonnes of mud and torrents of water slid down the hill carrying off houses and burying people alive. More than one thousand died or went missing, and thousands were left homeless, in one of the worst humanitarian disasters of recent years, in a country recovering from an outbreak of the Ebola virus in 2014 and, prior to that, decades of bitter civil war.

Freetown had been established in a spirit of utopian optimism in the late eighteenth century, as a home for freed slaves, though just how noble the motives were behind its founding remains contentious. The settlement was the brainchild of the natural historian and pioneering etymologist, Henry Smeathman. Born in Scarborough, North Yorkshire, Smeathman was sponsored by Joseph Banks and the Quaker philanthropist and botanist Dr John Fothergill, to travel to Africa and the West Indies in 1771. He was to spend roughly four years on the Banana Islands just south of Sierra Leone studying and collecting plants, insects and minerals. Insects and, in particular, termites, soon became his obsession.

On his return to Britain in 1781, Smeathman published a treatise entitled 'Some Account of the Termites, Which Are Found in Africa and Other Hot Climates', which saw him lauded as 'the father of termitology' in the drawing rooms and coffee houses of London. During the period that Smeathman spent in West Africa, the Banana Islands and nearby Plantain and Bunce islands were active in the British transatlantic slave trade. By the 1780s, the cause for the abolition of slavery was growing, advanced by the likes of Fothergill and Granville Sharp, the campaigner who successfully helped the runaway slave James Somerset obtain his freedom after being brought to London by his Boston owner. That case, known as the Somerset Ruling of 1772, appeared to outlaw slave ownership in England, if not in the colonies, where the ruling didn't become law until 1833, with the passing of the Slavery Abolition Act.

During the American War of Independence, many ex-slaves and runaways had joined the loyalist cause in the hope of acquiring their liberty as English subjects under common law. In the aftermath of the conflict, and along with other black people in colonies across the Americas and beyond, they fled to England, settling in large numbers in London. It was to ease the plight of these refugees that, in 1786, Smeathman put forward a scheme for a colony for free slaves. His proposal was for an anti-slaving settlement, a 'Province of Freedom' that would thrive through agriculture and commerce, its inhabitants by 'common consent' able to 'possess as much land as he or she could cultivate', and able to benefit from the spoils of their own labours. The intentions behind the plan are questioned by many contemporary historians, some of whom take it as a covert exercise in ethnic cleansing and an attempt to replace one mode of exploitation with another, but in its time it received the backing of prominent ex-slaves and abolitionists, including Granville Sharp.

Close to four hundred former slaves survived the passage to Sierra Leone in 1787, but delays to their departure ensured they arrived just in time for the start of the rainy season. Beset by the elements, dwindling stores, disease and disputes with the region's indigenous tribes, the settlement floundered and failed. It would rise again in 1792, when a fresh party of 'returnees' reestablished the settlement. They were known as the 'Nova Scotians', since the

majority were ex-slaves from North America who had taken refuge with the British in Canada and sailed from Halifax to Sierra Leone. The population grew substantially after the passing of Britain's first anti-slavery legalisation in 1807. In the following year, the British claimed Sierra Leone as a colony, and the country relinquished some of its liberty as a consequence. It was Britain's first colony in West Africa, and Freetown's mountain villages – York, Regent, Bathurst, Leicester and Gloucester – still bear English names. In retrospect and for all its flaws, in intention and execution, the founding of what became Freetown in 1787 arguably marked one of the first steps in bringing to an end the appalling forced migration of Africans across the Atlantic to work as slaves on the plantations of the North American colonists.

BELOW: The mountains that rise above Freetown supplied the country with its name – Portuguese navigators referred to the highest peak as Serra Lyoa (Lion Mountain). Transliterated into English, it became Sierra Leone.

FRESHKILLS PARK
USA
New York City

At this point in the twenty-first century, no vehicle is quite as orange as New York's Staten Island Ferry. The tubby little boat that travels from Manhattan to Staten Island is a deep, 1970s, sunburst orange; a super-8-film-stock orange; the orange of fizzy drinks before tartrazine was banned. The colour is even more pronounced against the sludgy green-grey of the Hudson River and the shiny towers of the Big Apple, and rather charmingly dated. If the farmers' market close to the port's entrance on the Manhattan bankside exemplifies a contemporary New York of bankers and loft apartments, with its array of expensive homegrown produce, boarding the boat still feels like stepping back in time. It's free, for a start. Then there is the view: as Manhattan island recedes, the sheer island-ness of the place becomes genuinely astonishing.

Staten Island is home to Fresh Kills, once the largest landfill site in the world. Named by Dutch settlers in the seventeenth-century, after the 'fresh waters' of what was a tidal creek on the western side of the island, Fresh Kills was marshland frequented by wading birds and blue crabs; a natural wetland across which flowering herbs blossomed. In time Staten Island was to serve both as a garden nursery and a beach retreat for the growing metropolis – a kind of short-hop Long Island – albeit one that, in the early nineteenth century, remained home to a quarantine station. Thanks to its swampy ground, Fresh Kills was also plagued by the occasional outbreak of malaria.

In the century that followed, New York City's park commissioner Robert Moses, alighted on Fresh Kills as the site for a new city garbage dump. A nondriver, Moses was New York's self-styled 'construction coordinator' and the master planner who was to run a six-lane expressway through the heart of the Bronx, eviscerating the borough in the process. His Fresh Kills scheme was pushed through in 1948 with the understanding that, after three

NEW JERSEY

ARTHUR KILL

Meredith
Woods

West Shore Expressway

Victory Boulevard

TRAVIS

William T. Davis
Wildlife Refuge

0   1000 yards
0   1000 metres

N

STATEN

Main Creek

Little Fresh Kills

Fresh Kills

East
Mound

Isle of
Meadows

FRESHKILLS   PARK

Richmond Avenue

Great Fresh Kills

former refuse
barge landings

Richmond Creek

South Mound

ISLAND

West Mound

South Park

Owl
Hollow
Fields

West Shore Expressway

Arden Heights
Woods

GREENRIDGE

ARDEN HEIGHTS

Covered trash mounds

years, these soggy grounds, once sufficiently desiccated by rubbish, would be redeveloped with housing for local people. As it was, the trash of Greater New York came first. By the mid-1950s, 27,200 tonnes (30,000 tons) of garbage were being ferried here from the city's five boroughs every single day. The stench from its acres of fetid detritus could, on breezy days, be smelt for miles around.

In the late 1990s, amid concerns about the impact of Fresh Kills on the environment, city officials agreed to close the site down. The final shipment of rubbish, including material from the World Trade Center, was deposited in 2001. Since that time, and following an arduous and not inexpensive process of capping dangerous waste, Freshkills (now one word)

BELOW: Looking back at the Manhattan skyline from Freshkills Park.

has gradually been 'rewilded'. Already unrecognisable as the near-toxic dump of old, its trash mounds are covered with meadows and grasslands. Raptors, grasshopper sparrows, owls, rodents, bats and butterflies have flocked to this revitalised ecosystem in droves, oblivious to its years in waste disposal. With a total area of close to three times that of Central Park, there is an ambition to transform Freshkills into both a habitat for wildlife and environmental conservation, and the largest open green public space in New York. Frederick Law Olmsted, co-designer of Central Park and one of the father figures of landscape architecture in America, was once a Staten Island resident and would surely have approved.

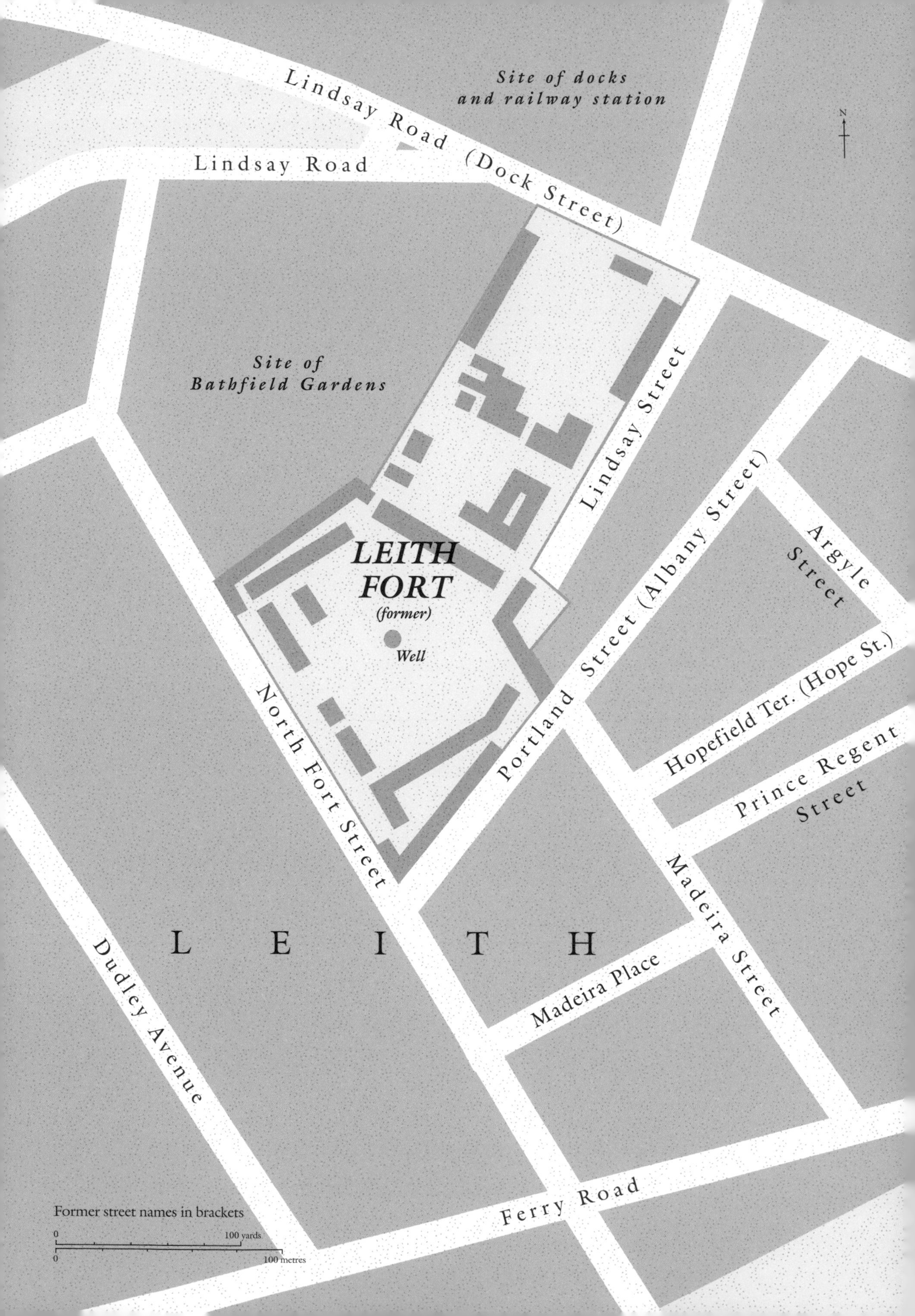

Site of docks
and railway station

N

Lindsay Road (Dock Street)

Lindsay Road

Site of
Bathfield Gardens

Lindsay Street

LEITH
FORT
(former)

Well

Portland Street (Albany Street)

Argyle
Street

Hopefield Ter. (Hope St.)

Prince Regent
Street

North Fort Street

L   E   I   T   H

Madeira Street

Madeira Place

Dudley Avenue

Ferry Road

Former street names in brackets

0		100 yards
0		100 metres

55° 58' 38.1" N 3° 11' 04.4" W

FORT HOUSE
SCOTLAND
Leith, Edinburgh

An Englishman's home is sometimes said to be his castle, a phrase dating back to the seventeenth century and a time when property was predominantly the preserve of males. The saying has roots in a statute of common law that gave homeowners the basic right to prevent unwelcome intruders from entering their abodes. But for the residents of a rather notorious 1960s housing estate in Leith, in the northeast of Edinburgh, the castle-ish-ness of their home was somewhat more than a figure of speech.

Lying at the mouth of the Water of Leith, on the blustery coastal shore of the Firth of Forth, Leith has served as Edinburgh's port for centuries. By the eighteenth century, it was a nexus for North Sea trade, its importance to British mercantile and maritime power underscored during the American War of Independence. In 1779, John Paul Jones, a Scot from Kirkcudbright who had helped found the American navy, sailed around the north coast of Scotland on a daring mission to capture Leith and hold the port to ransom. Lacking any kind of garrison, Leith was woefully undefended. As the seven-ship-strong American squadron sailed into view, a scratch militia of the town's fittest amassed on the harbour wall, to save face as much as anything, and everyone braced themselves for the inevitable defeat to follow. Edinburgh is known as the 'windy city' and its coastal outlier, Leith, one of its windier areas. By a remarkable quirk of fate, a high wind gusted in, stalling Jones's flotilla in the mouth of the Forth, eventually forcing him to abandon the attack. Leith breathed a sigh of relief, but vowed do something about its pitiful defences rather than rely on the weather to come to its rescue in future. Work on a fort for Leith was underway before the year was out, to a plan by James Craig, the architect behind Edinburgh's bold New Town, which had been designed to instantiate the Enlightenment principles of progress and rationality.

Initially, the fort comprised a battery of nine guns facing north in a half-moon formation, with large bastions to the southern side, and barracks. Enlarged during the Napoleonic Wars, when it was used to house French prisoners, it gained an outer boundary wall, guardhouses and a gateway. In 1824, gunners at the fort joined the battle to save Edinburgh from the flames of the Great Fire – the dreadful inferno that raged for four days, engulfing the historic Tron Kirk, Edinburgh's landmark parish church, and destroying some of the oldest surviving architecture in the city. An army base during the Second World War, Leith Fort was the long-term home of The Royal Army Pay Corps until 1956. After the departure of this unit, Edinburgh Borough Council earmarked the site for urban renewal.

Looking to rid the inner city of the back-to-back tenements it deemed backward and unsanitary, the council's scheme for the fort was to comprise a trio of stirringly modern tower blocks on the periphery. Their height – crowned by the twin towers of Cairngorm and Grampian House at twenty-one storeys apiece, and built by the firm of Miller – was intended to be emblematic of the council's ambition to lift the city's poor out of squalor. A large part of Leith Fort was demolished to make way for the development, but sections of its outer walls and two Palladian lodges were among several structures that were preserved, creating a surreal collision between the state-of-the-art and municipal and the aged and militaristic. One guardhouse was converted into a electricity substation, while another was repurposed as the concierge's office of the estate's central seven-storey block, Fort House.

From the mid-1970s, Scotland suffered enormous economic hardship. Unemployment doubled, and doubled again in the first half of the 1980s. One of Leith's biggest employers, the Henry Robb shipyard, closed in 1984. Joblessness, and its attendant social issues – along with an influx of cheap heroin from Pakistan, its prevalence in Leith in the early 1980s vividly chronicled in fictional form in Irvine Welsh's bestselling 1993 novel *Trainspotting* – contributed to the area's decline. The fort arguably fell hardest of all; plagued by drug abuse, crime and antisocial behaviour, it was frequently cited as the worst estate in Scotland. In 2013, Fort House, the last remaining block (Cairngorm and Grampian having been bulldozed in the 1990s) was finally pulled down. In its place stands a new development of low-rise houses, modelled after the 'Edinburgh colonies concept'. As different as they are to their brutalist predecessors, they too enjoy the protection of chunks of fort wall.

RIGHT: Forming part of the original development in the 1960s (top left), the fort's original Palladian lodges still feature in the 2017 refurbishment (top right), as do sections of the fort's outer walls (bottom).

46° 17' 50.5" N 44° 17' 52.4" E

CHESS CITY

Russia

Elista, Republic of Kalmykia

An enthusiasm for chess goes back centuries in Russia. Legend has it that Ivan the Terrible, the first Tsar of all Russia, died while playing chess. Peter the Great carried a board with him on all his campaigns and Catherine the Great found time to dabble in the game between romantic trysts during the course of her long reign. Following the revolution in 1917, this pursuit, beloved of Lenin and Trotsky, was taken up by the ruling communist party and promoted under the slogan 'Take chess to the workers!'. (Karl Marx, needless to say, had also adored chess. While living in impoverished exile in London in the 1850s, he would go on chess binges for days at a time.) Chess was played widely across the Soviet Union, its popularity stoked by the staging of the world's first international tournament in Moscow in 1925.

Shot during this landmark championship and boasting cameos by real players, the Russian silent film *Chess Fever* (1925), directed by Vsevolod Pudovkin, depicted the Russian capital in the grip of a mania for the game. A charming, lighthearted romantic comedy rather than a piece of Soviet agitprop, the film's plot revolves around a young man who is so obsessed with chess that he manages to miss his own wedding. Vladimir Nabokov, who, as an emigre in Berlin, augmented his earnings as a budding writer by selling chess problems, supplied another portrait of a Russian chess fanatic with his early novel *The Defence* (1930). Its protagonist Aleksandr Ivanovich Luzhin is a grandmaster scarcely able to function beyond the board, who ultimately loses himself to the game.

Since the end of the Cold War – a conflict waged as much through the nail-biting contests between American wunderkind Bobby Fischer and Soviet ace Boris Spassky, as through the race for nuclear arms and space supremacy – chess has had a lower profile. A torch for the game has been kept, nevertheless, in the self-governing Republic of

MOSCOW

Volga

KAZAN

OBNINSK

RYAZAN

Oka

TULA

SARANSK

ULYANOVSK

BRYANSK

R U S S I A

PENZA

Sura

OREL
(ORYOL)

YELETS

TAMBOV

LIPETSK

KURSK

VORONEZH

STARYY OSKOL

SARATOV

KHARKIV

Don

KAMYSHIN

U K R A I N E

DNIPRO

VOLGOGRAD

KAZAKHSTAN

LUHANSK

DONETSK

Volga

Don

VOLGODONSK

MARIUPOL

ROSTOV-ON-DON

Sea of Azov

ASTRAKHAN

**CHESS CITY,
ELISTA**

KERCH

KRASNODAR

STAVROPOL

Kuma

*Caspian
Sea*

CHERKESSK

SOCHI

C A U C A S U S

Black Sea

GRONZYY

0   200 miles

0   300 kilometres

GEORGIA

N

Kalmykia. Situatied on the northwest coast of the Caspian Sea, this remote scrap of bare steppe is roughly the size of Scotland and is one of Russia's poorest regions. Its people are Buddhists descended from nomadic Mongul herdsmen, who settled here in the seventeenth century. Their long tenure in these lands was not enough to prevent the Kalmyks being dispatched en masse to Siberia by Stalin in 1943, where as many as half died. The rest returned in 1957, only to discover that the collective farming methods forced upon them, and in particular the bulk import of the wrong type of sheep, were to play havoc with local agriculture, gradually reducing much of the fertile arable land to desert. Responding to this new terrain as best as they could, Kalmyks have, in recent decades, adapted to survive by breeding camels for their milk and meat instead of sheep. None of this, however, was to stop the region's wealthy post-Soviet president, Kirsan Ilyumzhinov, from funnelling millions of dollars (their sources not entirely accounted for and those funds perhaps more desperately needed elsewhere) into creating a world capital of chess in Kalmykia.

Chess-mad since childhood and the region's champion at fifteen years of age, Ilyumzhinov swept to power in 1993 while still in his thirties, on the platform that 'a wealthy president' was 'a safeguard against corruption'. One of his first acts was to make chess a compulsory subject in all of Kalmykia's schools. Appointed head of the International Chess Federation (FIDE) in 1995, Ilyumzhinov persuaded the organisation to bring the world championship to Kalmykia's capital, Elista, the following year. Its success spawned the dream of erecting a purpose-built chess facility – a whole Chess City, no less – on the dusty fringes of the city.

A stately Chess Palace in glass and steel would rise, flanked by a village of bungalows, a hotel, shops and a swimming pool, in time to host a Chess Olympiad in 1998. But the project faltered amid increasingly eccentric claims of alien abduction by Ilyumzhinov, a tightening of financial regulations under Putin and a growing unease over allegations by the international chess community, of human rights abuses in the region. An architectural model of the proposal remains on show in the lobby of the Chess Palace – a vision of rows of turreted buildings whimsically modelled after rook pieces. The Chess Palace and its surrounding facilities live on as a museum and as a venue for weddings, clearly for those not quite so obsessed with the game to forget their fiancées.

LEFT: A hotel complex in Chess City (top). Although there is talk of developing the site further (bottom), it has fallen largely into disuse since hosting the world's leading chess players in 1998.

FORDLÂNDIA
BRAZIL
Pará

I t is well documented that the automobile manufacturer Henry Ford was picky about many things – the type of people he employed mostly, but also food. Ford had grown up dirt poor on a farm in Dearborn, Michigan, in the American Midwest, and would go on to nurse a lifelong hatred of livestock, advocating their wholesale replacement with soybean substitutes. Some of Ford's own lunches on occasions consisted solely of wheat kernels that he had soaked until they were almost ready to sprout. He also snacked on dried kernels, tossing them into his mouth like peanuts to stave off hunger pangs, or when he was too busy to eat anything else. Regarding food as fuel, and the consumption of rich dishes merely wasteful of resources and energy, Ford once hoped to market a cracker made of oatmeal, wheat germ, pecans and olive oil that might do away with all other meals entirely.

It is perhaps ironic, then, to discover what the inspiration was behind Ford's most significant innovation, the moving assembly line, which he introduced in 1913. The process reduced the time it took to build a Model T from 12.5 hours to 1.5 hours and ushered in the new age of rapid bulk production and mass car ownership. Ford got the idea by seeing how a neighbourhood meat packing plant 'disassembled' its carcasses.

Ford made cars, but also saw himself as a maker of men (and women). In 1914, he was famed for bringing in a pay rate of 'five dollars a day' at his plants, almost twice the industry standard, and for an hour's less work than elsewhere. Such remuneration, he stated publicly, would ensure his workers could buy the cars they built, locking everyone into a mutually beneficial system. The reality was that, prior to declaring that rate, he'd struggled with absenteeism and had difficulty retaining staff, as workers loathed the monotony of the machine-like tasks performed. Like earlier and no less paternalistic employers, Ford believed that a happier, healthier and more responsible citizen could be bred from the factory floor

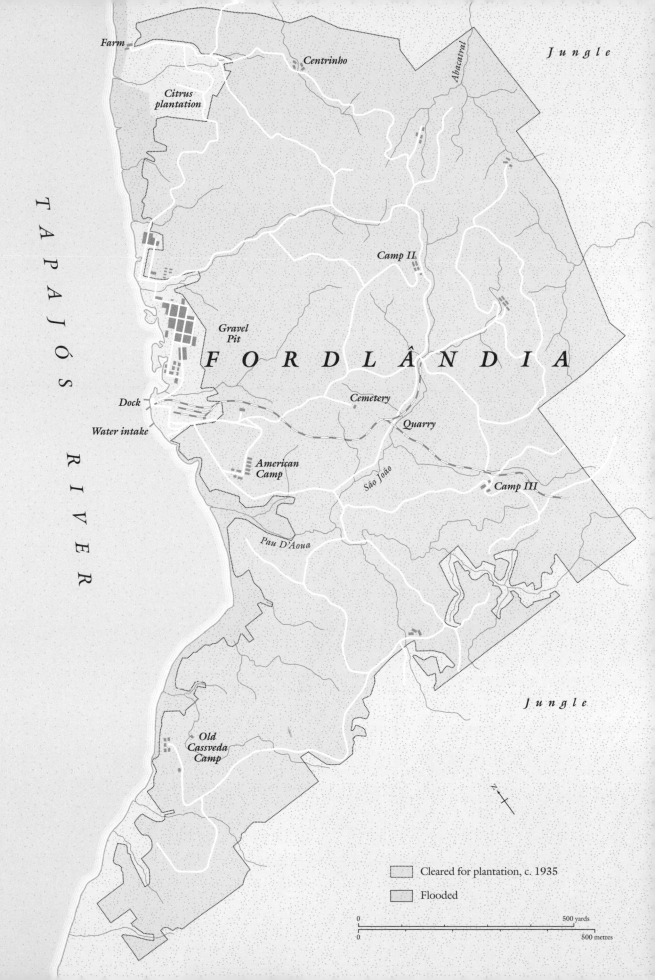

Farm

Citrus plantation

Centrinho

Abacatrral

J u n g l e

T A P A J Ó S   R I V E R

Camp II

Gravel Pit

F O R D L Â N D I A

Dock

Water intake

Cemetery

Quarry

American Camp

São João

Camp III

Pau D'Aoua

Old Cassveda Camp

J u n g l e

N

Cleared for plantation, c. 1935

Flooded

0   500 yards

0   500 metres

up; disciplinarian tendencies manifested as edicts against talking, singing or whistling at work. Ford's law didn't stop at the factory gates. For workers to qualify for higher rates of pay, their lives outside the plant had to be beyond reproach. The carmaker had a monitoring department with teams of agents who were sent to inspect employees' homes and interview neighbours to ascertain if they gambled, smoked, drank or neglected their families or failed to keep a tidy house. The distinction between the personal and the professional was blurred further still when Ford began to develop his own planned communities. After acquiring 126,000 hectares (311,000 acres) of timberland at Iron Mountain in Michigan, with the aim of increasing the company's self-sufficiency, Ford established a model industrial village around the sawmill and plant that processed lumber for the wooden automobile framework, floorboards and wheels.

Ford's interest in owning, operating and coordinating all the resources needed to produce complete automobiles did not stop there. In 1927, the same year that he opened his monolithic River Rouge industrial complex in Dearborn, he acquired 1 million hectares (2½ million acres) of land on the banks of the Tapajós River, a tributary of the Amazon River in Brazil, with the intention of securing a source of rubber for tyres, valves and hoses. At the time, British plantations in Ceylon (Sri Lanka) and Malaya supplied two-thirds of the global crude rubber production. However, new trade restrictions threatened to raise

the cost of rubber sold to America by tens of millions of dollars a year. The answer, as far as Henry Ford was concerned, was not only to grow his own rubber in Brazil, but also to plant an ideal Midwestern American town there, to serve as a beacon to progress and the morally improving possibilities of his particular brand of capitalism. Fordlândia was to be the town's name – a pleasant Main Street kind of place of tidy ranch homes with modern plumbing, neat sidewalks lined with red fire hydrants, schools, shops, a sawmill, a water tower, a hospital, tennis courts and a golf course.

With the local conditions largely unsuitable for the cultivation of rubber trees, with caterpillars and lace bugs and leaf blight rife, the project was doomed from the start. Fordian attempts to ban alcohol and impose a diet of oatmeal, canned peaches and brown rice resulted in a full-scale riot, as aggrieved employees vented their fury at changes to the canteen facilities. Malaria, yellow fever and venereal disease ran wild. The community unravelled and Ford's grandson Henry II finally disposed of it in 1945 at a massive loss, selling it on to the Brazilian government for $244,200: the Ford Motor Company had invested something close to $20 million up to that point. Overgrown with weeds and reverting to nature, today much of Ford's Fordlândia appears remarkably similar to the areas of Michigan and the Midwest that helped spawn it, and lies just as desolate in the rainforest as its cousins in Detroit and elsewhere in the rust belt.

BELOW: Two derelict rubber factory buildings stand facing each other in the middle of Ford's, now desolate, town.

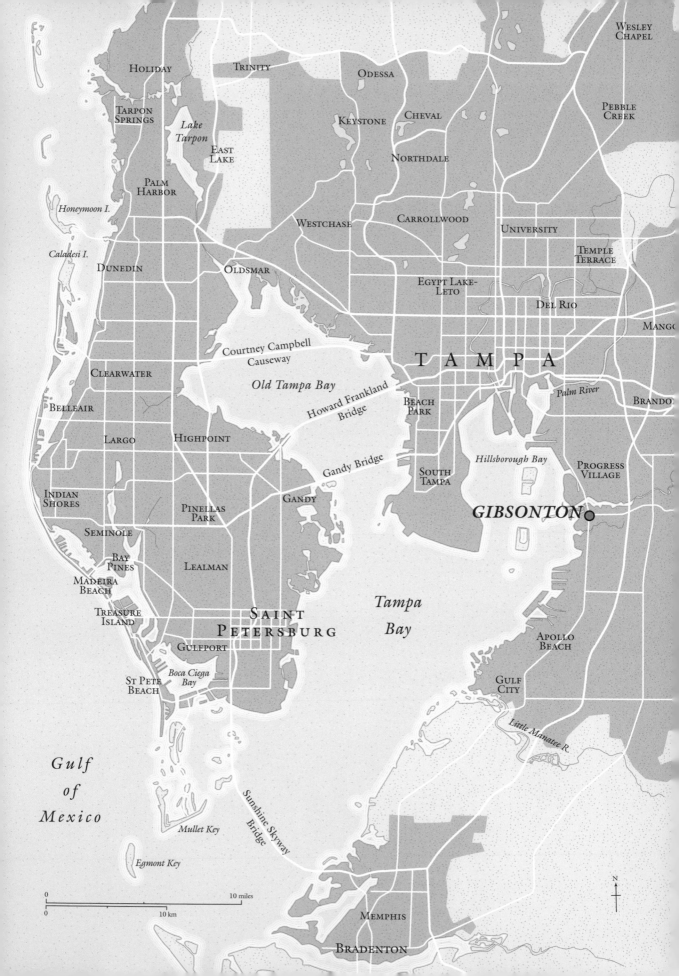

27° 50' 56.0" N 82° 22' 54.1" W

GIBSONTON

USA

Florida

The formal numbering of interstate highways in the United States dates from the 1920s. With Henry Ford's mass-produced Model T having put car ownership within reach of millions of Americans, the demand for decent roads had seen miles of ragged dirt track replaced by smooth tarmac, itself laid with Fordian mechanical efficiency. Initially, the nation's burgeoning network was a confusing mess, with the names of its major arteries – and the signs needed to negotiate them – varying from region to region, state to state, county to county and, on occasions, from mile to mile. The federal government stepped in to bring order and uniformity to the whole system, insisting upon the use of generic signage and supplying a batch of numbers for the highways: even figures were applied to those routes going east to west, and odd figures to those running north to south.

Highway 41 was among the first tranche of these state-spanning American routeways. The course of this 3,200 km (2,000 mile) road ran, and continues to run with a few curtailments and rerouting here and there, north to south from Michigan's Upper Peninsula and Lake Superior right down to the Everglades and Miami. As such it passed, and still passes, through the states of Michigan, Illinois, Wisconsin, Indiana, Kentucky, Tennessee and Georgia before arriving in sun-kissed Florida. Since its inception it has offered those wishing to avoid the brutal winters of the Midwest (and only Minnesota ranks worse than Michigan in that respect) a corridor to gentler climes. Today those making this pattern of migration are commonly known as 'snowbirds', and the sight of a fleet of modern SUVs heading south has fast become as reliable an indicator of the changing seasons as the appearance of swallows in the skies up above. Decades before them, this path was beaten by America's show people and carnival folk; the fairground operators and the artists whose circuses and sideshows toured up and down the country – a band of travellers for whom the hard surface of Highway 41 was both a lifeline and a way of life. With the summer winding down, and with audiences for performances under canvas and in big tops dwindling, the show people tended to look for somewhere to hole up for the quieter and colder months.

Some time in the 1930s, news began to spread of the perfect campsite at a place called Gibsonton, 20 km (12 miles) outside Tampa, Florida. Close by the Alafia River, the campsite's banks were lush with oak and sabal palms and its waters teeming with fish. Its owners were The World's Strangest Married Couple – a show duo whose 'Big' Al Tomaini stood at 2.4 m (8 ft) tall and 'Little' Jeanie Tomaini at just 75 cm (2½ ft). The couple had been tipped off about Gibsonton by a fellow show act, 'fat lady' Ruth Pontico from Tampa. At the time, Gibsonton's population stood at little over six hundred, most of them fisher folk or employees of a nearby lumber mill. The show couple wintered there contentedly for several years, before purchasing 1.4 hectares (3½ acres) of riverfront land and establishing the Giant's Fishing Camp. The first left turning off Highway 41, the location was supposedly chosen from a lifetime of observing how fairgoers naturally veered left when entering the halls. Performers rather than punters migrated to Gibsonton (or Gibtown as it was soon known) in their thousands, finding true fellowship in a place where Al the Giant served as camp proprietor as well as the local police and fire chief, and the fruit stall was run by the famous Hilton siamese twins. Catering to the unusual needs of its diverse inhabitants, the town was quite unique. Under a special zoning law, for example, residents were allowed to keep and train exotic animals and store fairground equipment on their front lawns – it's a tradition that carries on to this day, although the number of active performers has diminished. For the most part, Gibtown now looks like a fairly ordinary American town, with a gas station, a library and a Walmart store. The only hints of its glorious fairground heritage lie in the occasional pile of rusting amusement ride parts and the odd gaily painted trailer here and there.

The likes of Al and Jeanie, and acts such as Emmett 'the alligator skin man' are long gone, as are the lion-tamers, bearded ladies, fire-eaters and tattooed musclemen, and with good reason. Yet the International Independent Showmen's Association retains its headquarters in Gibtown. And glasses are regularly raised to the memory of the artistes who put it on the map at the Showtown Restaurant and Lounge Bar, a venue that doesn't lack outlandish performances on its own regular karaoke nights, as it is.

RIGHT: The Showtown Restaurant and Lounge Bar, with its faded facade (top). Circus memorabilia on display at Gibsonton's International Independent Showmen's Museum (bottom).

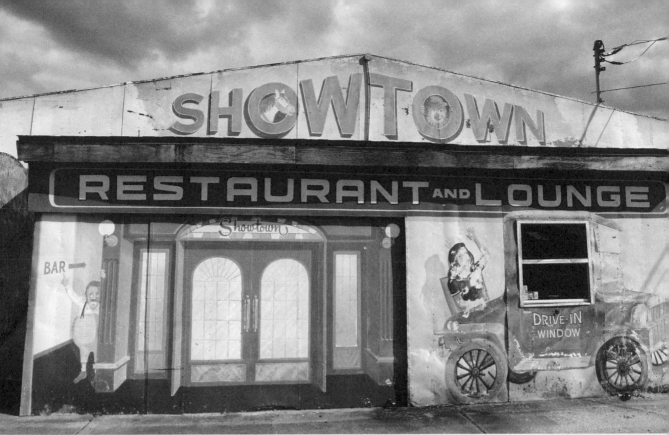

50° 04' 18.9" N 20° 02' 14.7" E

NOWA HUTA
POLAND
Kraków

Since at least the creation of Eridu (modern-day Tell Abu Shahrain) in Mesopotamia, in around 5400 BC, people have lived in cities. The dream of building the perfect city as the ultimate expression of humankind's imagination has been with us since Hippodamus laid out the Athenian port-city of Piraeus in ancient Greece, to a plan with a regular grid of streets. In Renaissance Italy, such orderly classical schemes were revived with the underpinning principle that the erection of such places would improve the inhabitants' lives, both physical and morally. In 1593, the Venetians constructed Palmanova, a fortress city on the northeastern frontier of the mainland, to defend against attacks from the Ottoman Turks. Designed in the shape of a nine-pointed star, with a central piazza, its plan was the work of the empire's brightest architects and military engineers. These were men of rigour and reason, who dreamt of a metropolis that functioned with the order of a well-drilled platoon and that reflected the larger society at its best, with clerics, merchants and artisans all contributing to its stratified, if hearty, civic and economic life. Unfortunately the petite bourgeoisie found its immaculate streets and rigid form too austere for their tastes.

It is, perhaps, a pity that neither Joseph Stalin and the Soviet Polish government nor Tadeusz Ptaszycki, the chief architect behind Nowa Huta, the planned Soviet city built 10 km (6 miles) outside Kraków, in Poland, in the late 1940s, didn't study the history of Palmanova more closely before embarking on their own ideal city. As one commentator has observed, Nowa Huta is so loaded with bizarre contradictions it seems more like something from a dystopian science-fiction novel than a real place. The adjective 'Orwellian' is not infrequently deployed in descriptions of it.

Nowa Huta was intended to stand as a Soviet showcase and to act as an ideological and architectural affront to Kraków, with its medieval buildings and rather well-to-do

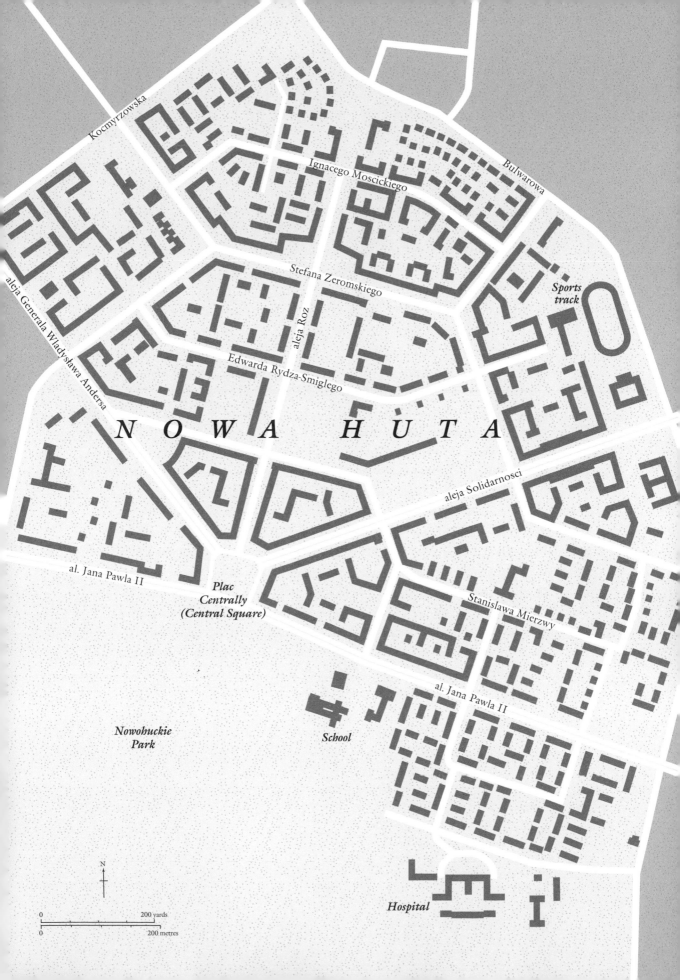

Kocmyrzowska

Ignacego Moscickiego

Bulwarowa

aleja Generala Władysława Andersa

Stefana Zeromskiego

aleja Roz

Sports track

Edwarda Rydza-Smiglego

N O W A   H U T A

aleja Solidarnosci

al. Jana Pawla II

Plac
Centrally
(Central Square)

Stanislawa Mierzwy

al. Jana Pawla II

Nowohuckie
Park

School

N

Hospital

0   200 yards

0   200 metres

cosmopolitan mores. The city's name simply means 'New Steelworks'. The aim was to impose, from scratch, a self-consciously working-class community of industrial labourers on Kraków's doorstep. The whole grand project hung on what was to become the biggest steel plant in communist Poland – the Vladimir Lenin Steelworks. That there was no iron ore or coal for hundreds of miles, and pretty much everything needed to produce the steel had to be imported in bulk from elsewhere in the Soviet bloc, was only a minor inconvenience.

Thousands of workers from across Poland were invited to help build Nowa Huta, so forging a 'bright future' for themselves, each with the promise of a shiny new apartment for their labours. If not to everyone's liking, for arrivals from the poor peasant villages of the eastern borderlands, these newly constructed buildings were a notable improvement on the rural homes they'd previously lived in. Construction was carried out at a furious pace, with the plans being rubber-stamped in May 1947, and the first apartment block completed in the summer of 1949. Quite deliberately echoing Renaissance models, the city was laid out in a monumental sunburst patten with great wide streets fanning out like rays from the central square. From 1973, until its destruction in 1989, a monumental statue of Vladimir Lenin stood at its north end. The father of the Russian Revolution was omnipresent, his vast features gazing down from on high as if keeping a vigil over the city as a whole, though seemingly not dissuading vandals from attacking the stonework in later years.

In keeping with Lenin's own anti-religious doctrine and Soviet ideological orthodoxy, Nowa Huta was designated a 'town without God' with no churches or places or symbols of worship to be built in its environs. This issue proved extremely contentious, with the erection of a cross at one point leading to violent clashes between the citizens and the authorities. Far from fostering pliant worker bees in a perfect hive, Nowa Huta seemed to breed dissent and, in the 1980s, its residents and the local steel workers were at the forefront of the anti-Soviet Solidarity movement, campaigning for free speech and staging the strikes that would ultimately help hasten the end of communist rule.

Although much of Ptaszycki's scheme was never completed, Nowa Huta clearly shows what can be done with a plan, the will and the means. Whether such order is entirely humane remains a moot point. Its form commands the eye and inspires admiration but, like any relic of authoritarianism, it also slightly chills the heart.

RIGHT: Plac Centralny (Central Square; top). Originally named in honour of Joseph Stalin, Nowa Huta's main square later took Ronald Reagan's name for a brief period. The People's Theatre (bottom).

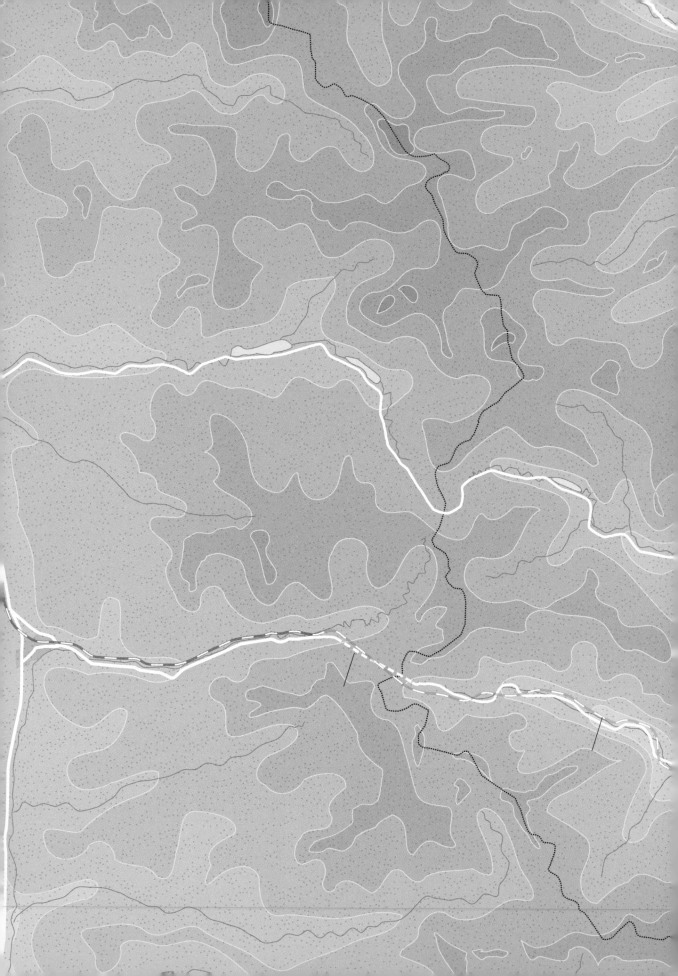

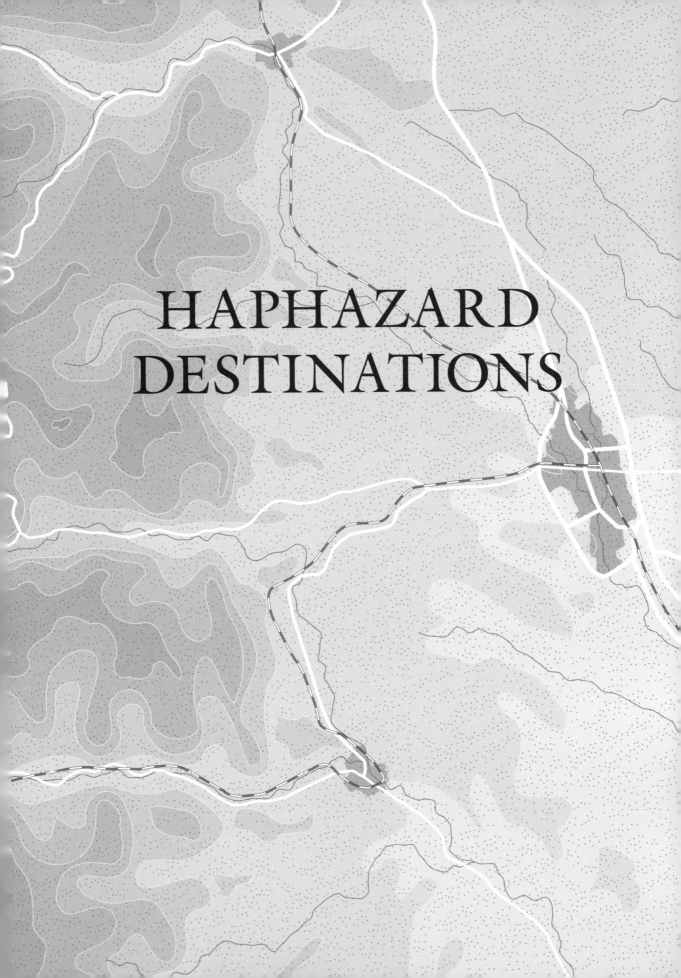

HAPHAZARD
DESTINATIONS

NEFT DASHLARI

AZERBAIJAN

Caspian Sea

Fire and water are the supreme symbols of purity in the ancient Iranian (formely Persian) faith of Zoroastrianism, one of the world's oldest extant religions. Fire represented the light of God and the illuminated mind. It was – and continues to be – a central component of all Zoroastrian rituals and ceremonies. Zoroastrian fire temples, their interiors iridescent with eternal flames, were promoted with the spread of the Persian empire, which at its greatest extent *c.* 480 BC ranged from Egypt or Macedonia in the west to modern-day Afghanistan and Pakistan in the east. Among its many territories was an area encompassing modern-day Azerbaijan, situated beneath the Caucasus Mountains and beside the landlocked Caspian Sea. The Persians hailed it as 'The Land of the Holy Fire', for here were deposits of a highly flammable oil that bubbled up from beneath the ground unbidden and kept the Zoroastrian temple fires blazing.

The Muslim Conquest of Persia, which culminated in about AD 651, spelled the demise of Zoroastrianism as the main faith of the Persian people and, by the nineteenth century, Azerbaijan was under Russian rule. In 1878, when the Russian-Swedish arms and oil moguls Robert and Ludvig Nobel were scratching around for a name for the very first oil tanker to ferry supplies of 'black gold' from their refineries near the Azerbaijan capital of Baku, across the Caspian Sea and up the Volga for distribution across Russia and beyond, they chose to call it *Zoroaster*. This single ship was to revolutionise the transport of oil, and turned Baku into one of the leading centres of its production and export; by 1900, its wells were supplying half of all the oil in the world.

In the wake of the Second World War, Soviet engineers tasked with maximising oil production to aid the rebuilding of the shattered towns and cities of the Eastern bloc began drilling at a reef some 70 km (45 miles) east of Baku, and far out in the Caspian Sea.

On 7 November 1949, they hit pure crude oil over a 1,000 m (3,280 ft) deep beneath the seabed and hurriedly established the first offshore oil platform above it. Further drilling revealed this was not a one-off occurrence, and it was not long before the number of platforms grew, to pilfer at this distant outpost. The development was somewhat haphazard, the pillars of the platforms supported on the remains of seven capsized shipwrecks, among them the hulk of that first tanker, the *Zoraster*. In time, the number of rigs rose to more than 2,000, all linked together via a chaotic network of steel and timber bridge-roadways some 3,500 km (2,200 miles) in length, and along which battalions of trucks thundered to and fro. Also perched out over the ocean on these structures were apartment blocks, a factory, shops, a cinema, a park and a football pitch. This expansive floating metropolis was dubbed Neft Dashlari, or Oily Rock. At its peak, it was home to some 5,000 people. Like the occupants of more naturally occurring islands, the inhabitants were fiercely loyal to their offshore dominion, its vulnerability to the forces of nature and the up to twelve-hour voyage back to the mainland only sharpening a genuine sense of comradeliness.

With the fall of the Berlin Wall and the break-up of the Soviet Union, Neft Dashlari's fortunes plummeted. Oil prices were at the mercy of the global open market and fresh fields offered easier pickings for petroleum speculators. If still a productive oil field today, much of Oily Rock looks decidedly rocky. A mere 45-km (28-mile) sliver of its once ingenious expanse of bridge roadways is accessible. The rest lies rusting out of reach, or has been carried off entirely by the wind and the sea. With its oil deposits estimated to last just twenty years longer, only unlikely sounding plans to refurbish the site as a hotel – long discussed but, as yet, no nearer to realisation – may prevent those elements from claiming entirely what remains before long.

ABOVE: With a workforce of some 2,500,
the 'streets' of sprawling Neft Dashlari trail
as far as the eye can see.

NILE

Teraat Gazirat   Badran

GEZIRA ISLAND

Nile Corniche

Shobra

Al Sabtiah

Al Teraa Al Bolakia

Emtedad Ahmed Helmi

Port Said Street

6th of October Bridge

Ramses Street

El-Abaseya

RAWD AL FARJ

Ramses Street

EL-ZAHER

El-Gaish

26th of July St.

6th of October Bridge

Talaat Harb

EL-GAMALEYA

Salah Salem Street

Tahrir Square

Noubar Street

Port Said Street

Kobri Al Ebageah

C A I R O

GARDEN CITY

Nile Corniche

MANSHIYAT NASER

Rubbish dump

AL ABAJIYYAH

EL-SAYEDA ZAINAB

Magra El-Eyoun

Al Khelaa

Kobri Al Ebageah

AL MUQATTAM

MAJRA AL UYUN

Salah Salem St.

EL-IMAM EL-SHAFEI

Al Fostat Street

Al Khayala

N

FUSTAT

Nile Corniche

0   1 mile

0   2 km

30° 02' 10.1" N 31° 16' 42.6" E

MANSHIYAT NASER

EGYPT

Cairo

It says as much about Manshiyat Naser or 'Garbage City' that, to reach it, you must first pass through the City of the Dead. The names of these places are about as achingly literal as they can be. The City of the Dead may not be a city exactly (and neither, technically, is its near neighbour the Ville des Ordures), nor are all of its inhabitants these days dead. But it is, or was, a graveyard.

In more recent times, this outlying cemetery has been built on, colonised by the living, who have been priced out of Cairo itself. In a similar vein, the streets of Manshiyat Naser are littered with rubbish – hence its name. Garbage City is a checklist of lacks. There is no electricity here. The water supply is patchy and sanitation and drainage poor. Most of the apartment blocks, shops, eateries and municipal buildings are unfinished or falling down. Rubbish is the lifeblood of the settlement, and festering bags of it fill whole warehouses, open yards, alleyways, front rooms and practically every spare space in which it can be stashed and picked over for anything recyclable. Half of all the rubbish in Cairo ends up at Manshiyat Naser, transported by lorry, car, horse and trap, donkey and cart, lone camel and by hand. At the time of writing the population of the Egyptian capital stands at around 9.5 million people. It is not difficult to imagine the amount of waste they generate.

To the credit of the Zabbaleens (rubbish collectors) – by far the majority of Manshiyat Naser's inhabitants — some 85 per cent of the garbage that arrives here is recycled and sold on. A reasonable living can be had on trash, but life is far from easy here. Ever-present ambient pollution and rats are just some of the hazards. Another is the fact that the majority of the Zabbaleens, around 90 per cent, are Coptic Christians, who, as a religious minority, have suffered discrimination. Their choice of occupation is partly historical: in years gone by, and in a predominantly Muslim country, rag-picking was frequently one of the few trades left open to them. However, the bulk of the Zabbaleens living at Manshiyat Naser seemingly descend from peasant farmers who gravitated towards Cairo from Upper Egypt following a spate of poor harvests in the 1930s and 1940s. At first, they did their best to raise livestock on the fringes of the city but found trash a more sustainable option in the end. Those Christians who farmed pigs, whose consumption is expressly forbidden in the Qur'an, duly put them to work by feeding them perishable waste. In 2009, during fears of a global pandemic from the H1N1 virus (swine flu), the Egyptian government ordered the mass slaughter of Cairo's pigs, almost all of which were to be found in Manshiyat Naser. Violence duly flared in the settlement, as residents resisted the authorities' heavy-handed attempts to impose a ruling that disproportionately affected the livelihoods of the Coptic minority.

Whatever crosses the inhabitants of Manshiyat Naser have had to bear since, the Cave Church of St Simon the Tanner Monastery is a defiant symbol in this detritus-strewn suburb. This mega-church shaped like an amphitheatre is built into the side of the Mokattam Mountain and can hold up to 20,000 people around a central pulpit. As the largest church in the Middle East, its presence so close to scenes of such squalor, if nothing else, is a reminder of the power of faith.

RIGHT: Covering an estimated 5.5 km² (2 sq miles), Manshiyat Naser has a population approaching 60,000.

47° 47' 50.2" S 73° 32' 00.3" W

CALETA TORTEL

CHILE

Capitán Prat Province

A resinous, aromatic, coniferous evergreen, the cypress tree was adopted as a symbol of life by the ancient Persians; among Buddhists and disciples of the Japanese Shinto faith, it remains sacred and is often cultivated near pagodas and temples. In many cultures, however, the cypress is most closely associated with mourning. That connection stems, in part, from the ancient Greeks and their mythical account of the unhappy demise of Cyparissus. The son of Telephus and the most beautiful boy on the island of Cos, Cyparissus was adored by Apollo, while he, himself, doted on a magical pet stag. One day, while out frolicking in the forest with this animal, Cyparissus accidentally mortally wounded it with his bow (or javelin according to some versions of the tale). Overcome with grief, the boy vowed to die himself and wept until all that was left of him was a dried-up husk. Apollo, unable to bear this once handsome boy looking so forlorn, duly transformed him into a tree – one whose wood is light, easy to work with and extremely durable. This last quality led to cypress wood being deployed in the manufacture of coffins. It was widely believed across many faiths, that the resistance of this timber to decay enhanced the chances of immortality for those interred within.

Situated at the junction of two ice fields at the mouth of the Baker River and an inlet to the Pacific Ocean in southernmost coastal Patagonian Chile, Caleta Tortel definitely feels poised between life and – if not death – certainly the end of solid land. Topographically this corner of Chile hovers between land and sea and ice and water. The Baker River is named after Admiral Sir Thomas Baker, the British naval commander in charge of the South Pacific station at the time of Charles Darwin's second voyage on HMS *Beagle*. It is the largest river in the country and famed for its turquoise hues, caused by the mineral deposits in its bed and banks. The landscape here is all fjords, inlets and islands. Climactically, dampness in the form

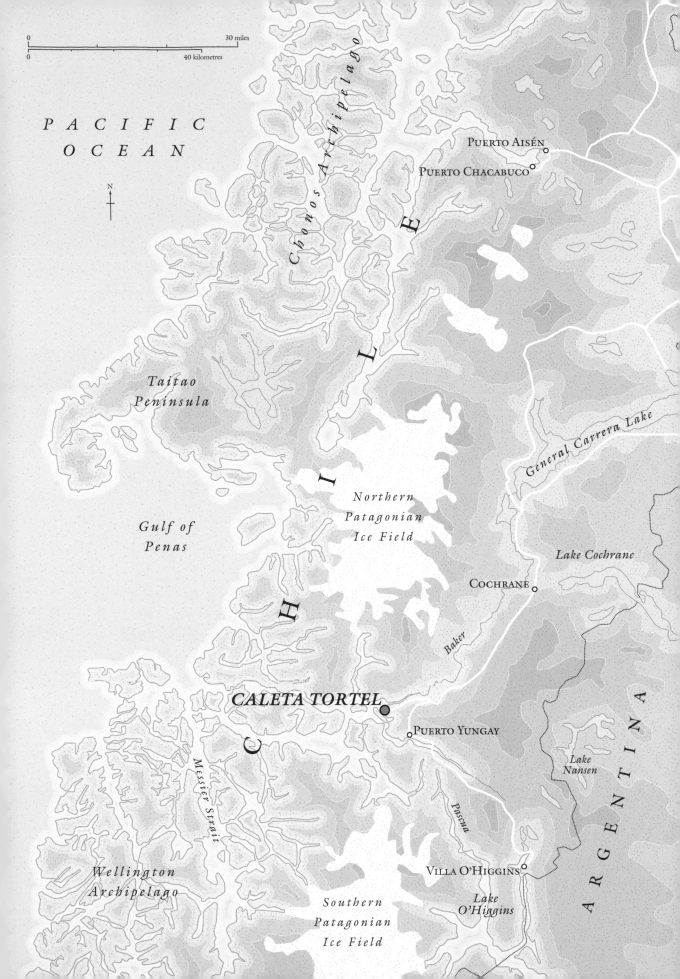

PACIFIC
OCEAN

N

Chonos Archipelago

PUERTO AISÉN
PUERTO CHACABUCO

C H I L E

Taitao
Peninsula

General Carrera Lake

Gulf of
Penas

Northern
Patagonian
Ice Field

Lake Cochrane

COCHRANE

Baker

CALETA TORTEL

PUERTO YUNGAY

Messier Strait

Lake
Nansen

Pascua

A R G E N T I N A

Wellington
Archipelago

VILLA O'HIGGINS

Lake
O'Higgins

Southern
Patagonian
Ice Field

0   30 miles
0   40 kilometres

of persistent mist and chilly rain predominates. The region is also home to abundant cypress forests. Caleta Tortel itself is less a village than a collection of crazy, vertiginous planking that was almost willed into existence in 1955 by the Chilean navy, in order to make the most of the local cypress lumber. Logging, alongside fishing and tourism, sustains this tiny coastal community still, whose population runs to just over 500. There are two churches, one Catholic the other pentecostal, and a primary school. Adolescents are dispatched to Cochrane – a metropolis of more than 2,000 people and a three-hour bus ride away – to continue their high-school education.

There is, however, no getting away from cypress at Caleta Tortel. In this precarious-looking village, all of the houses, the stilts on which they stand and the walkways that connect them, are made from the wood. There are no roads: a 23-km (14-mile) gravel track that nudges up to one end of the settlement, linking it to the Carretera Austral highway, was only completed in 2003.

As a peculiar hotchpotch of teetering wooden huts and, often, extremely steep boardwalks truly on the edge of solid ground, Caleta Tortel, nicknamed 'the Venice of Chile', has a particular allure. Currently lacking Wi-Fi, and with just one, single phone line, and fresh water and electricity supplies rather at the mercy of the elements and an unreliable turbine, the village is indeterminacy writ large. As such, it is also perceived by many as a haven from much of modern life.

RIGHT: The village of Caleta Tortel scales the steep mountain slope that rises from the bay. Boardwalks fringe its coastal extremity, while steep wooden stairs weave upwards from one tier to the next.

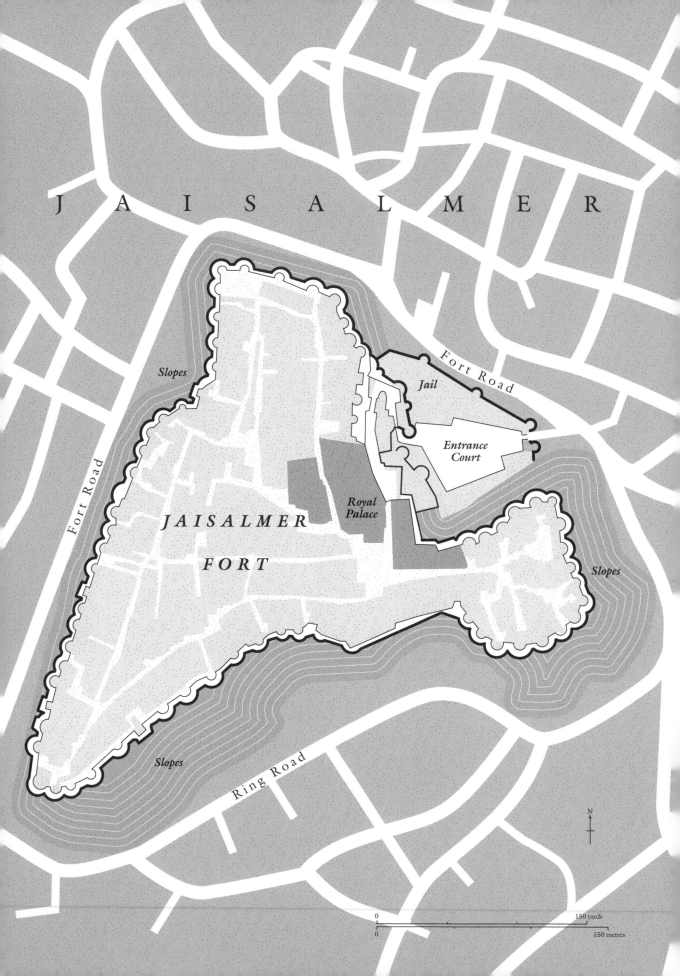

JAISALMER

Slopes

Fort Road

Fort Road

Jail

Entrance
Court

JAISALMER

Royal
Palace

FORT

Slopes

Slopes

Ring Road

N

| 0 | | 150 yards |
| 0 | | 150 metres |

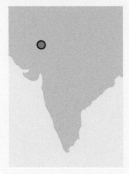

JAISALMER FORT

INDIA

Jaisalmer, Rajasthan

You would probably have to be quite a trusting soul to act upon the advice of a mystic hermit who suggested you should build a whole new fortress city on top of a hill in the middle of a desert judged so unforgiving that it is known as the abode of the dead. However, this is seemingly what initiated the creation of Jaisalmer Fort in the barren, far northwestern corner of Rajasthan, the Indian desert state that borders Pakistan.

According to a legend recounted in the epic Indian poem the Mahabharata, the Hindu deity Krishna prophesied that a great citadel would be founded on the top of the triangular, triple-peaked hill of Trikuta. In 1156, hearing this story from a hermit called Eesaal, the powerful ruler of the Rajput tribe of warriors and traders, Rawal Jaisal, wasted no time in attempting to make good the god's prediction. A combination of its founder's name and that of the Meru – the unassailable mythical mountain of the Gods – Jaisalmer rose high and grand. Its stately royal palaces and quarters were augmented by temples and lavishly decorated marble-walled mansions commissioned by the statesmen and wealthy merchants who gravitated to the fortress court.

Encircling the entire city was a concentric ring of defensive walls, built in the rich yellow-red sandstone unique to the quarries of the Rajasthan region. A peculiarity of the stone at Jaisalmer is that its colour varies according to the position of the sun in the sky. The walls shift in hues from light yellow to blood orange during the course of the day, reaching a dazzling gold in the late afternoon – a tone that led to the fort being popularly dubbed Sonar Kella or the Golden Fortress. Approaching the fort today, as it simmers in the sun in such a distant, desolate location, Jaisalmer appears almost mirage-like; the incongruousness of its presence here, in the Thar desert, is enough to make beholders of the vision doubt their own eyes.

Somewhat out of the way today, in Rawal Jaisal's day, the city was on the Silk Route that passed through India on its way from China to the Mediterranean, and served as a hub for trade and a stopping-off point for passing travellers. Its importance declined with the opening up of sea routes and, subsequently, the building of railways under British rule, but the city is far from a phantom. It is a rare example of an actively inhabited fortress city; with some 2,000 residents, it claims the title of India's last 'living fort'.

It was Satyajit Ray, the great Bengali film director and novelist, who arguably helped put Jaisalmer on the global tourist map. He used the fort in one of the hugely popular detective yarns he wrote for young adult readers featuring the Kolkata private investigator, Prodosh Chandra Mitra, aka Feluda. In 1974, he adapted the book for the big screen. The resulting film, *Sonar Kella*, a Hitchcock-style adventure for children, was shot mostly on location and became one of his most commercially successful movies. Its enduring place in the collective memory of successive generations of Bengalis raised on the movie and the Feluda stories, has ensured that East Indians make up one of the largest single groups to visit Jaisalmer Fort.

Having survived sackings, invasions, the rise and fall of several empires and a number of earthquakes (the most recent in 2001), however, Jaisalmer's walls and buildings have been gradually crumbling away, a process that has accelerated in recent decades. The decay is thought to result from water seeping into the fort's foundations, themselves composed of weak sedimentary rock. The source of the water is the city's ageing sewage system, which is now struggling to cope with the increasing volume of water sluicing through it. Much of the water – something in the region of 225,000 litres (50,000 gallons) every day – is imported by the local hotels and restaurants rushing to meet the demands of ever-increasing numbers of visitors to the city. At the time of writing, a variety of preservation schemes and preventative works are being undertaken to ensure Jaisalmer stands every chance of surviving for another eight hundred years.

ABOVE: Perched on its hill above the Thar Desert, Jaisalmer is one of the world's few remaining inhabited fortress cities.

JUST ROOM ENOUGH ISLAND
USA

St Lawrence River, New York

What do the words 'thousand island' bring to mind? A dressing, most likely. One usually made from mix of mayonnaise, ketchup and pickles and herbs, pre-packed bottles of which sit pink and bitty, and congealing slightly in chill cabinets the world over. But the namesake of this gloopy salad topper, is a real place. As it happens, the Thousand Islands, at 1,864 in total, are closer to 2,000 and squat in the St Lawrence River between New York and Canada.'.

At the turn of the twentieth century, this upper New York state archipelago, just 595 km (370 miles) north of Manhattan, came into vogue as a secluded summering spot for the millionaire industrialists of America's Gilded Age. Railway mogul George Pullman, the Kellogg family of breakfast cereal fame and George Boldt, owner of the Waldorf Astoria hotel, all had properties here. Boldt liked the place so much he had two holiday homes, one on Wellesley Island and the other on the heart-shaped Hart (later Heart) Island. On the latter, he wasted no expense building a mansion styled after a Rhineland castle for his wife, with a heart motif incorporated into its architectural detailing. Sadly Mrs Boldt died in 1904, calling a halt to construction and Boldt was never to visit the island again.

According to one story, the Boldts were partially responsible for the invention and subsequent popularity of thousand island dressing. One fine morning, the couple were out cruising on their steam yacht on the St Lawrence Seaway. As lunchtime approached, the Boldt's chef discovered that the onboard kitchen lacked the ingredients necessary for dressing the couple's prerequisite salad. (Fresh greens themselves were then undergoing a boom among the East Coast moneyed, who forked out for pricey iceberg lettuce, freighted in from California on newly refrigerated train cars.) He opted to improvise using the condiments to hand, adding a diced boiled egg for good measure. Having delighted the

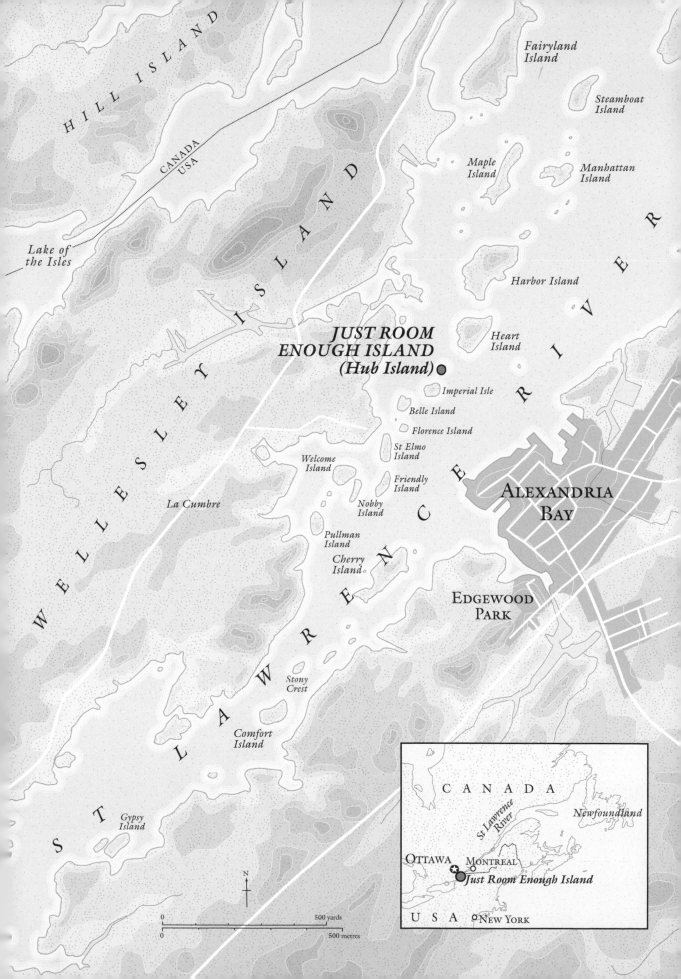

HILL ISLAND

CANADA
USA

Lake of
the Isles

Fairyland
Island

Steamboat
Island

Maple
Island

Manhattan
Island

Harbor Island

W E L L E S L E Y   I S L A N D

**JUST ROOM
ENOUGH ISLAND**
(Hub Island) ●

Heart
Island

Imperial Isle

Belle Island

Florence Island

*St Elmo
Island*

Welcome
Island

*Friendly
Island*

La Cumbre

*Nobby
Island*

*Pullman
Island*

*Cherry
Island*

S T   L A W R E N C E

R I V E R

**ALEXANDRIA
BAY**

**EDGEWOOD
PARK**

S T

L A W R E N C E

*Stony
Crest*

*Comfort
Island*

*Gypsy
Island*

N

0   500 yards

0   500 metres

C A N A D A

St Lawrence River

Newfoundland

OTTAWA ☆

Montreal ●
Just Room Enough Island

U S A   ○ NEW YORK

Boldts, the resulting mayonnaise-based concoction found its way onto the Waldorf Astroria's menu as 'thousand island dressing', taking salads by storm the world over.

Whatever the true provenance of the dressing, for other stories abound, it is no longer the preserve of super-rich salad eaters. You could say the same is true of the Thousand Islands, now overtaken by the Hamptons, Cape Cod and Palm Beach as bolt holes of choice for supremely affluent Americans, yet it remains a pretty select kind of place. To this day the majority of the islands in the archipelago are privately owned – some in the hands of the same families who bought them over a century ago.

The appeal is obvious: who doesn't dream of an island to call their own, particularly when that island happens to be in a rather scenic, fashionable, socially desirable spot where the climate is kind, the fishing not bad and mainland civilisation only a short boat ride away? Where better to while away a weekend or a few weeks in the warmer months, after all? Certainly the Sizeland family, on seeing Hub Island in Alexander Bay in 1950, were swept away with such notions. At around 300 m² (3,200 ft²), Hub Island was – and is – one of the retreat's smallest island. It is about the size of a modern American home, which is just as well because that is exactly what the aptly named Sizelands built on it: a single house for holidaying in, with a tree and a fence for some privacy. There was just room enough for that and nothing more; and Just Room Enough was the title they bestowed on their property once the house was completed. Gazing out across the water at their nearest neighbour, Heart Island, and at the remnants of Boldt's Castle, they could only congratulate themselves on the good sense and modesty of their own scheme, while pondering the extravagance of earlier generations.

Today both houses have become objects of fascination. Boldt's Castle presently operates as a tourist attraction run by the Thousand Island Bridge Authority. As such, it has helped put Just Room Enough Island on the visitor map affording, as it does, the best views of the Sizeland family's lilliputian island kingdom – currently estimated to be the smallest occupied island in the world.

LEFT: The Sizeland's house looks precarious sitting on Hub Island. There is literally just room enough for a table and a few chairs beside the water's edge.

SPIEGELHALTER'S JEWELLERS

ENGLAND

East London

Aristide Boucicaut and his wife, Marguerite – milliners and fabric merchants – started modestly enough in 1838, selling lace, ribbons and buttons on Paris's Left Bank. In 1852 the couple branched out, opening a shop called Le Bon Marché or The Good Market. Despite a few earlier contenders for the title, among them Harding, Howell & Co's Grand Fashionable Magazine, established on London's Pall Mall in 1796, it was the world's first proper department store. An all out, everything-under-one-roof affair, it stood as the original *grand magasin* teeming with an array of goods that shoppers could peruse at their leisure. Business boomed and it moved to new premisses at 24 rue de Sèvres, in the 7th arrondissement, in 1869. Three years on, the Boucicauts were forced to expand again, this time seeking the expertise of the engineer Gustave Eiffel, in time of the tower fame, and the architect Louis-Auguste Boileau to refashion their building accordingly.

The inspiration for the emporium at the heart of Émile Zola's 1883 novel *Au Bonheur des Dames*, Le Bon Marché continues to trade as a purveyor of reassuringly expensive haute couture to well-heeled Parisians, and much else besides. Back in the day, this mode of commerce was much imitated in London, often slavishly. In 1876, James Smith, an inveterate gambler who'd made good on the horses at Newmarket, chose to funnel his winnings into retail. He set up a department store on near identical lines – he even called it Bon Marché – on the Brixton Road in South London. The same concept would travel across to the United States, where two years later, Macy's in New York first opened its doors, advertising itself as 'The Great Sixth-Avenue Bazaar: A Place Where Almost Anything May Be Bought'.

By the 1880s, such familiar names as Harrods, Harvey Nichols and Liberty were up and running in London, but it wasn't until the flamboyant Wisconsin-born retailer George Selfridge opened his store at the western end of Oxford Street in 1909, that

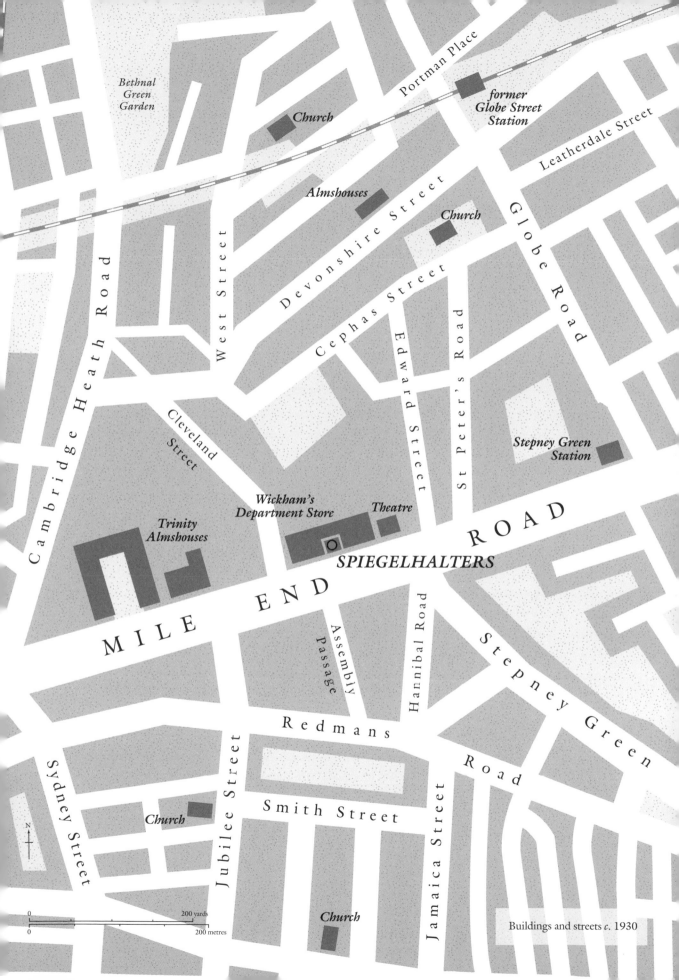

Bethnal
Green
Garden

Portman Place

*former
Globe Street
Station*

Church

Leatherdale Street

Almshouses

Church

Devonshire Street

Cephas Street

Cambridge Heath Road

West Street

Edward Street

St Peter's Road

Globe Road

Cleveland
Street

*Stepney Green
Station*

**Wickham's
Department Store**

Theatre

**Trinity
Almshouses**

SPIEGELHALTERS

M I L E   E N D   R O A D

Hannibal Road

Stepney Green

Assembly
Passage

R e d m a n s

Road

Sydney Street

Jubilee Street

S m i t h   S t r e e t

Jamaica Street

Church

Church

N

0   200 yards
0   200 metres

Buildings and streets *c.* 1930

Londoners became true fans of the department store. A dazzling beaux-arts palace, with hundreds of departments, a roof garden, restaurants and reading rooms, its floors filled with knowledgeable assistants trained in the dark arts of politely making a sale, Selfridges combined classical elegance and New World glamour with cold hard commerce; it melted hearts and opened wallets in convincing numbers.

Eyeing the American's venture with interest from the other side of London was a draper, a Mr Wickham of Whitechapel, who set himself the goal of creating 'a Selfridges for the East End'. He had started to buy out neighbouring shops on the Mile End Road, and hired the architect Thomas Jay Evans to furnish him with a scheme to replace the whole terrace, running from numbers 69 to 89, once he'd acquired it. Evans' design was grand, ancient and modern in the beaux-arts Selfridges vein, with Doric columns and a monumental clocktower as it centre. It was also eagerly anticipated by those who believed it would improve the area no end. There was just one snag: a single shop, Spiegelhalter's jewellers at number 81, refused to sell up.

Spiegelhalter's was a family firm, built from scratch by Otto Spiegelhalter, a German immigrant who'd arrived in London in 1828. The Spiegelhalters had been trading on the Mile End Road since 1880 and had moved once already, in 1892. They'd seemingly had a tough time during the First World War. With anti-German sentiment running high, they had chosen to anglicise their surname, becoming Salters. The shop, however, still traded as Spiegelhalter's, and no matter what inducements Mr Wickham offered, the Salters would not budge and steadfastly held out against a sale.

Faced with such an obstruction Wickham had no option but to build his whole store around the remaining shop. The sweep and symmetry of Evans' original scheme was to be brutally compromised: on completion, in 1927, the central clocktower had been shunted to one side, and the shop's grand frontage rudely, and crudely interrupted by the presence of Spiegelhalter's stunted two-storey building.

Hailed by the great architectural writer Ian Nairn as 'a perennial triumph for the little man', this intransigent jeweller's shop became a much-cherished landmark, a monument to mice that roar and the brilliance of bloody-minded nonconformity. The story doesn't end there, however. Unable to keep up with the changing trends in retail, the arrival of supermarkets and Swinging London boutiques, Wickham's department store closed down in the 1960s. Spiegelhalter's, on the other hand, outlasted the store by nearly twenty years, closing in 1982. A redevelopment of the whole site is imminent, and following public outrage that this historic architectural oddity might be lost for ever, guarantees have been made that the remaining lower facade of number 81 will be retained in the new scheme.

ABOVE: Spiegelhalter's shabby shopfront
has become an architectural landmark in its
own right, described by Nairn as 'one of
the best visual jokes in London'.

36° 41' 15.7" N 23° 03' 23.6" E

MONEMVASIA

GREECE

Laconia

AEGEAN SEA

Harbour

GEFIRA

Monemvasias-Krokeon Road

Causeway

Monemvasias-Neapolis Road

Harbour

Locally, this site is known simply as Kastro, or the castle. Officially it is Monemvasia, which translates as 'the place with a single entrance'. To the Germanic Franks, who laid siege to it for a full three years in the mid-thirteenth century, it was Malvoise. For the English, who established a lighthouse here in the late 1800s, and who were partial to the local wine, it was Malmsey. Yet, at first glance, most visitors journeying along the narrow causeway towards this ancient fortress town on an islet at the southeastern side of the Peloponnese, can be forgiven for doubting there is much here at all.

Fittingly, perhaps, it was the ancient Greek philosopher, Aristotle, who provided an early discussion of camouflage in the natural world in his *Historia animalium*, when he wrote about the ability of octopuses to conceal themselves by changing their colour to blend in with their surroundings. With similar guile, the sight that Monemvasia immediately presents to the world is a fist of rock. An impressive enough fist of rock, granted, and one that was first separated from the mainland during an earthquake in the third century AD. Majestic and craggy, its jagged cliffs rise several hundred feet above the pellucid waters of the Aegean Sea, whose greeny-blue saline waves can, on stormier days, slosh and lash below with the

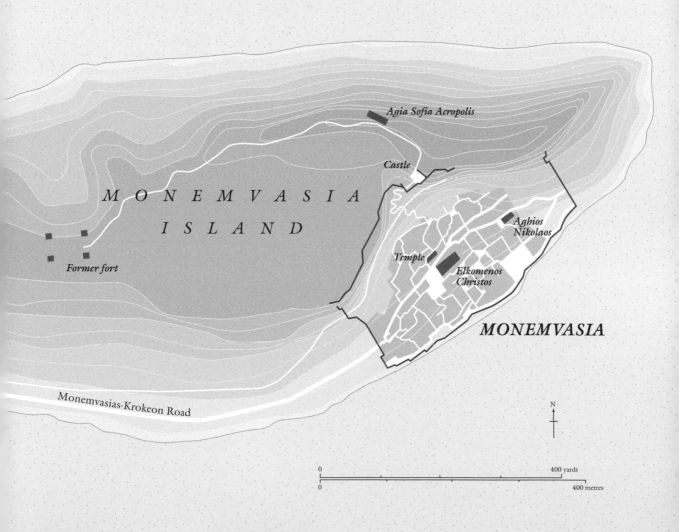

vehemence of the furies. Since fresh water is something Monemvasia lacks, storms – or, at least rain – are rather more welcome here than on some of the other islands in the Aegean.

From the causeway, a long, winding road eventually reaches a few outlying buildings and a vast external stone wall of forbidding appearance. A single narrow archway serves as the town's main, and only, gateway. Just large enough for a donkey and mount, it does a convincing job of dissuading the uninitiated from venturing any further. Pass through this meagre doorway, however, and a kind of architectural Aladdin's cave unfolds; a time-bending, two-tiered settlement, the lower half of which has remained occupied since the twelfth century. The main town retains the original fortifications, winding cobbled streets, churches, monastic buildings, and stone houses of the medieval era. Added to them, are the remnants of later religious institutions – including a former Ottoman mosque from the sixteenth century – and smart merchant's townhouses dating from the nineteenth century, with wrought-iron balconies. Up a raking hill lies the abandoned upper town, much of which languishes in splendid ruination, aside from the beautifully preserved Byzantine church of Agia Sophia.

Once of great strategic and military and mercantile importance, Monemvasia is a palimpsestic place in which the imprints of Byzantine, Venetian, Vatican, Ottoman Turk and modern Greek rule – even war-time occupation – are discernible from wall to wall and street to street. The fact that motor cars were unable to penetrate the age-old outer defences, could easily have sent the town into decline following the Second World War. Equally, and in more recent decades, mass tourism could have despoiled the place completely. Instead, restrictions on road traffic bolstered the growth of Gefira across the causeway – as a place of residence for the indigenous population, but also as a town with the space to accommodate more touristic amenities – leaving Monemvasia to concentrate on preserving the heritage on which it now trades quite healthily, and that it keeps securely secreted behind its walls.

ABOVE: Sheer cliffs rise hundreds of metres above the medieval town, obscuring it from the mainland.

UROS FLOATING ISLANDS

PERU

Lake Titicaca, Puno

Lake Titicaca is the largest lake in South America, its shores high up in the Andes mountains lapping at the borders of Bolivia and Peru. It is also home to around sixty floating islands, made of reeds woven together like giant mats and bound with clod to anchor them to the riverbed. The floating is to be expected – it is upfront and in the billing – as is the sheer insularity of these man-made islands. That these islands also happen to be edible is, perhaps, the more unexpected element here.

Although, just how surprisingly floaty these islands are shouldn't be downplayed entirely. The experience of stepping onto one of them can be compared to mounting a severely underfilled waterbed; they do drift about, and quite a bit. Still, the roots from the self-same totora reeds that bestow these artificial islands with their essential insularity also comprise part of the regular bill of fare in these parts. They can be eaten raw and have a texture and flavour not dissimilar to marrow or cucumber.

The floating islands in this region of South America are not that ancient, but they are old enough that their origins are largely mythical and seemingly impossible to verify. Although the true story may never be unravelled entirely, there is one version that is repeatedly – and obligingly – rolled out for the ever-rising tide of international visitors to the lake. It runs along the lines that follow.

There was once a unique ingenious people called the Uros, who migrated to the lakeside of Titicaca perhaps more than 3,000 years ago. If, finally, reaching an uneasy compromise with the nearby Aymara, with whom they eventually mixed and intermarried, the Uros spent many centuries as an ostracised ethnic group. Their position became especially hazardous with the arrival of the Incas, and they responded by retreating far into the lake on pontoons of their own imaginative construction. This did not save them from being seized as slaves

AYABACAS ○

PUSI ○

L A K E

JULIACA

T I T I C A C A

CANCHI GRANDE ○

PABLOCUCHU ○

Rio Ranis

CARACOTO

Capachica Peninsula

HUATA ○

CAPACHICA ○

Amantani

PUCAMAYO ○

r e e d   b e d s

Rio Ilpo

LLACHON ○

Lake
Umayo

PAUCARCOLLA ○

UROS FLOATING ISLANDS ●

Chucuito Peninsula

CALLANACA ○

PUNO

JAYLLIHUAYA ○

CHUCUITO ○

PUTINA ○

PLATERIA ○

0 ————————————————— 10 miles
0 ————————————————— 10 km

N

by the Incas from the mid-1400s, neither did it prevent them suffering the abuse of Spanish conquistadors later on, during the sixteenth century, but it did create the one-off society of ersatz island dwellers that persists today.

Home to around 1,000 self-sustaining inhabitants, the Uros floating islands lie within easy reach of Puno, the region's major city, and have become a well-trodden destination on the backpacking trail through the Andes. For outsiders, the novelty of the islands themselves is only enhanced by a topping of traditional huts and structures – including a watchtower – all of them ingeniously woven from reeds. For the islanders, however, this seems to have locked them into a kind of Sisyphean bargain with their chosen environment, since their floating lands rot away at a rapid pace and have constantly to be patched and repaired in

order to stay afloat. After a month or two, depending on the season, each island has to be abandoned as work starts on replacing it, this in turn succumbing to the inevitable forces of entropy and the elements, and so the never-ending cycle continues.

Meanwhile, the modern world gradually intrudes into the near timeless life at Lake Titicaca. The islanders, to the disquiet of conservationists, have readily embraced tourism, offering tours and accommodation (some of it quite swish, bolstered with solar power and contemporary mod cons). The Uros themselves parade in their traditional costumes and purvey handicrafts, seeing it, rightly perhaps, as a means of avoiding being exploited by someone else and securing a more certain future for themselves.

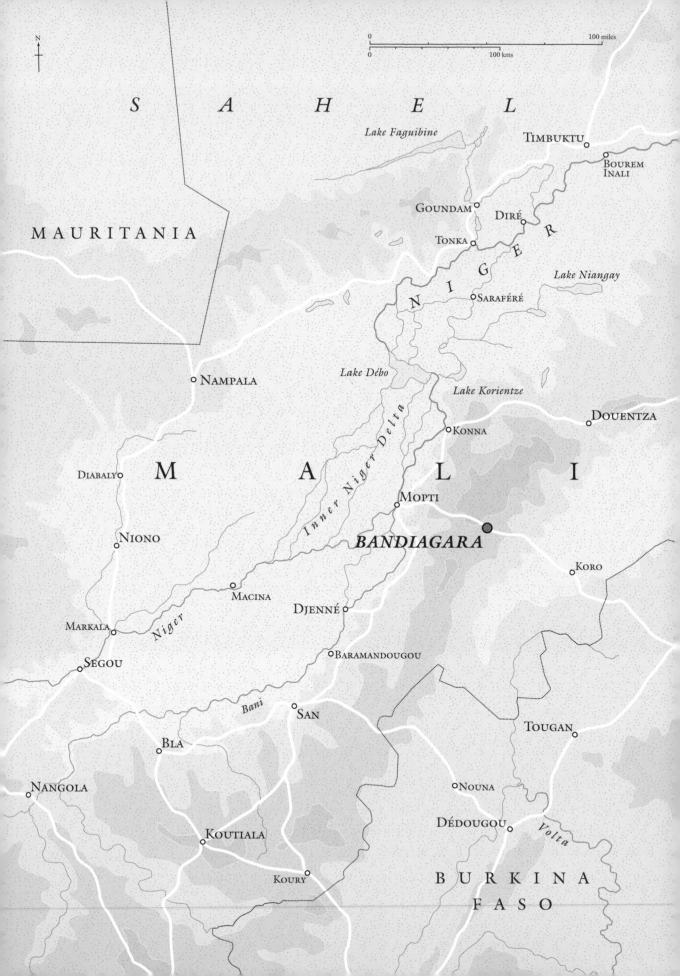

14° 25' 39.4" N 3° 19' 32.2" W

CLIFF OF BANDIAGARA
MALI
Mopti

Archaeologists suggest that the Bandiagara escarpment, an epic sweep of sandstone cliffs that runs for over 150 km (90 miles) across the arid, semidesert plains of the Mopti region of Mali in West Africa, has been occupied for over 2,000 years. The first settlers are thought to have been Toloy people, who were then succeeded by the Tellem. Little is known about either civilisations. Obscure relics have been unearthered, and it is thought that the Tellem initiated the building of the otherworldly earthen dwellings and burial chambers that are characteristic of the region, and that were subsequently colonised, and adopted, by the Dogon people following their arrival here in around the fifteenth century.

Widely taken to be among the most ancient of Africa's civilisations, Dogon people celebrate a culture that is grounded in clannish familial tribal loyalties, ancestor worship and animism – the belief that places, people and objects possess a distinct spiritual essence. As an oral society with no written records, quite how and why the Dogon came to inhabit this part of Mali, or exactly where they came from, is shrouded in obscurity. There is some speculation that they fled here from the south, possibly Ghana, either to avoid enslavement by Songhai, Fulani and Mossi tribesmen, or to avoid forced conversion to Islam. Whatever their own roots and their reasons for moving here, the Dogon rapidly displaced the hunter-gatherer Tellem from Bandiagara. Having gained control of the breadth of the cliffs, the Dogon dug in and started farming, raising millet and creating gardens in the patches of fertile ground between the stony precipices, and cultivating rice in rock pools. They took full advantage of their loftier position and the ready supply of boulders and loose stones that could be launched as missiles from above, to defend themselves against all would-be aggressors – a strategy that held good for at least four hundred years.

RIGHT: The earliest dwellings of the Bandiagara escarpment are those of the Tellem people. Wedged within crevices in the cliffs, they were built between the eleventh and fourteenth centuries.

It wasn't until the 1930s that anthropologists began to take an interest in the Dogon people. Before that time, the remote locality and fierce insularity of the Bandiagara escarpment and its immediate environs had ensured near isolation from the rest of what was then French-ruled Sudan. Few people in the West even knew of the Dogons' existence. It was arguably only when photographs of Dogon villages with their striking earthen buildings started to be published in the postwar period in such popular magazines as *National Geographic* and *Time*, that the world at large began to appreciate the ingenuity of these people. The Dogon granaries – stovepipe-like mud structures topped with thatch – are

one of the most distinctive features of their settlements. Others include the Togu Na – a special low-roofed hall used for public meetings. There are also a number of religious shrines and sanctuary houses (permanent residences for the spirits of the Dogon's more mythic ancestors), their walls heavily decorated with symbols.

Since 1989, the Bandiagara escarpment, with its 289 Dogon villages, has been listed by UNESCO as a World Heritage Site. While ecotourism adds to the local economy, today, resources from it are funnelled into helping the Dogon sustain their settlements for the benefit of their forebears and the generations to come.

6° 38' 34.5" S 140° 08' 20.9" E

KOROWAI TREEHOUSES

Indonesia

Province of Papua

It was in 1974 that scientists hacking their way through the dense foliage of the tropical rainforest of southeastern Papua New Guinea first reported making contact with the Korowai people. It is thought that they had lived in almost complete isolation until that point, remaining blissfully unaware of the world outside. To this day, there are Korowai clans to the north and further into the rainforest, who shun contact with strangers; many of them believe that outsiders carry demons and evil spirits with them. The Korowai adhere to an ancient and complex religious belief system that holds that the dead can return to the land of the living at any time and that people can be taken over by a *khakua*, or witch. Because of this, the Korowai people long practised cannibalism, convinced that killing and eating a person was the only way to counter demonic possession and banish evil spirits, although most anthropologists suspect that the practise has now stopped.

There are an estimated 4,000 Korowai still living in tight, hunter-gatherer communities in a relatively small area of swampy rainforest in the Upper Digoel Region of the Indonesian province of Papua, some 150 km (90 miles) inland from the Arafura Sea. With an annual rainfall of around 500 cm (200 in), it is one of the wettest places on Earth, its muddy forest floor and thick foliage play host to lethal microbes, poisonous spiders and deadly snakes. The Korowai have traditionally made their homes in gravity-defying treehouses some 40 m (130 ft) above the sodden ground. This preference for high living seemingly developed from a need for protection from rival clans as much as a desire to stay out of the way of nonhuman predators. At the heart of each house is a sturdy banyan tree. Once the tree's top is removed, the trunk acts as a central pole. A roof, floors and walls are then fashioned from the bark and woven leaves of sago palms. The cabin-like structure is then divided into two or three rooms, supported on anything from four to ten wooden silts. It can only be entered via a ladder.

The sago tree not only supplies the bulk of the material for the treehouses, but forms a main part of the Korowai diet, along with bananas. The tree's starchy centre is turned into a kind of flour that provides the ballast or binding agent in almost all the dishes prepared. Sago grubs, a good source of protein, are another staple. Every family maintains a small garden at the foot of its treehouse for cultivating sweet potatoes, vegetables and tobacco, while grasses, sugar cane and other edible plants and seasonal fruits and berries are foraged for in the forest. Only the men hunt and fish. With dogs, and using only primitive bows and arrows, they track down wild pigs and cassowaries, although they also catch small birds, snakes, lizards and rodents for the table.

Exposure to the outside world has inevitably brought change. Visited by scientists, missionaries and sightseers, many of the Korowai have come to an accommodation with outsiders. Some offer performances for tourists for a fee or sell small goods and trinkets in order to acquire machine-powered tools that their ancestors did without for so long. Increasingly, younger members are opting to leave the depths of the forest and live in villages along the banks of the Becking and Pulau (Eilanden) rivers. Only time will tell how much longer their age-old ways of living in the canopy of the forest will survive.

ABOVE: Each dwelling houses up to fifteen people consisting of a man and his wife, or wives, and their unmarried children.

PACIFIC OCEAN
Mussau Island
Admiralty Islands
Manus
Kavieng
New Ireland
Wewak
Bismarck Sea
Rabaul
Sepik
Karkar
PAPUA NEW GUINEA
Long Island
Central Range
Wabag
Mount Hagen
Mendi
Goroka
New Britain
Umboi
Lae
Kikori
Solomon Sea
Kerema
Owen Stanley Range
Fly
Gulf of Papua
Daru
D'Entrecasteaux Islands
Tufi
PORT MORESBY
Abau
Alotau
Cape York
Coral Sea
Cape York Peninsula

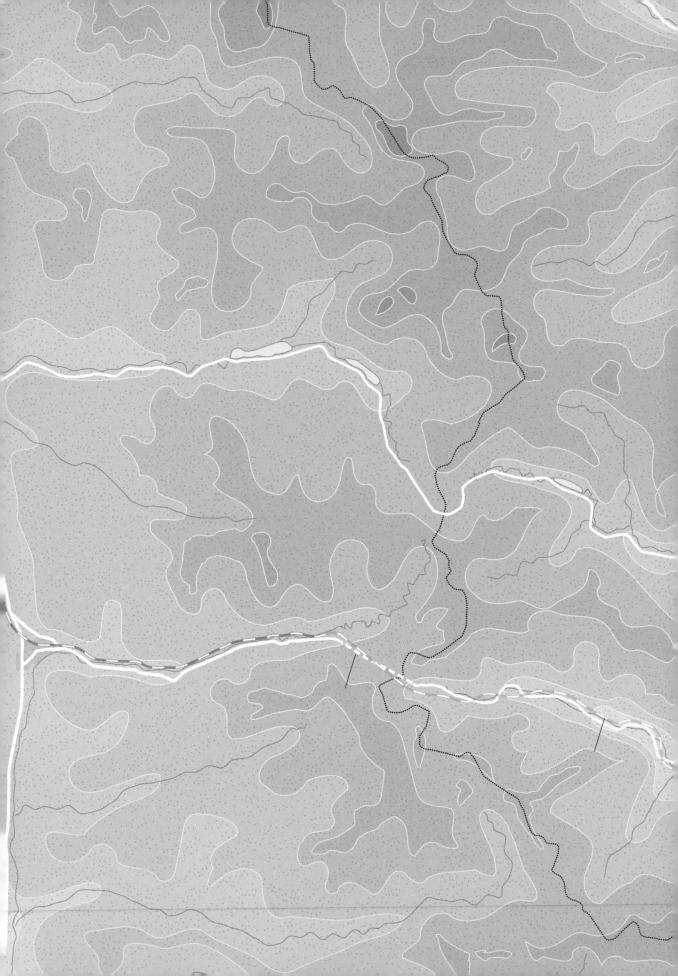

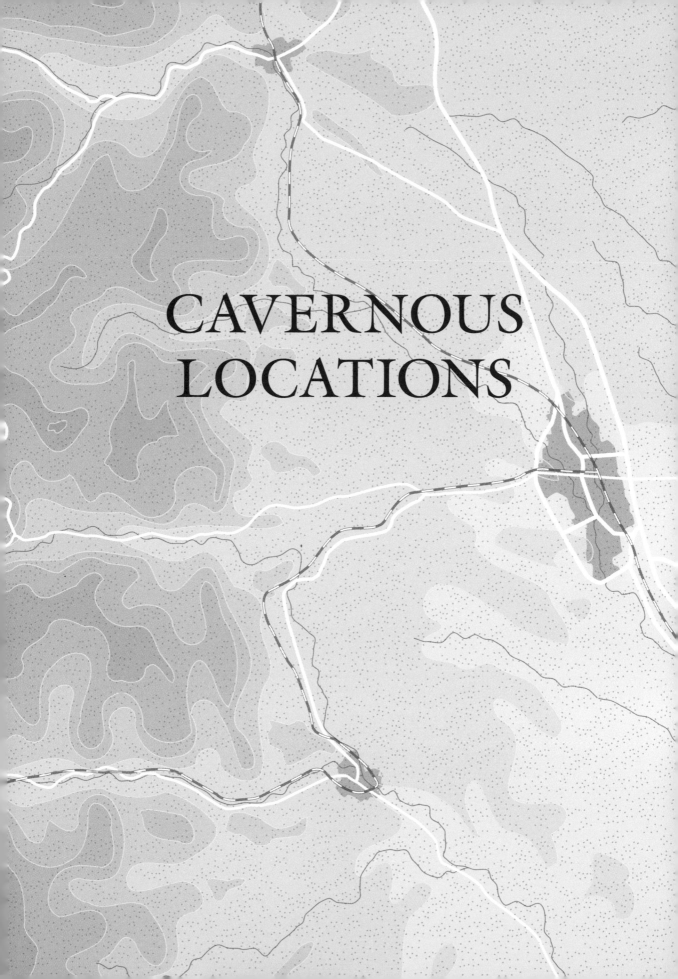

CAVERNOUS
LOCATIONS

LASCAUX CAVES
FRANCE
Montignac

Wrapped around the eponymous river that twists and turns through a landscape of green meadows and rocky hills, the Dordogne, in southwest France, is a region that could have been invented to fit the romantic ideal of the bucolic – and the Gallic. It is dotted with charming unspoiled villages that could only be French, with their grand chateaux, rough-stone hillside forts, farms seemingly of some pastoral yesteryear and extensive vineyards. As in Bordeaux to the west, viniculture is a way of life in the Dordogne, its Bergerac, Montravel and Pécharmant wines among the better-known varieties. One thing that all wine-producing regions of France have in common is that they were nearly wiped out entirely by the arrival of the aphid-like bug known as *phylloxera* in the 1860s. Unknowingly imported with American vines, this pest feasted on the roots of French vines with the result that entire vineyards turned yellow, drooped and died. A cure for the 'wine blight' was only found in the 1890s, with the development of a new, bug-resistant hybrid, that was created by grafting French vines onto American rootstocks. The nation's wine industry had escaped annihilation.

However, the breakthrough came too late for the vineyards on the hills of the Lascaux estate above Montignac sur Vézère, a picturesque riverside village on the eastern side of Dordogne with a ruined castle, ancient stone bridge and a smattering of late-medieval buildings. At Lascaux the decision was taken to replace the vines with pine trees. Shortly before the outbreak of the First World War, one of the pine trees became uprooted, exposing a gaping hole in the ground. The estate hands did their best to patch the hole up to prevent cattle falling into it and, soon enough, brambles took root on the spot, further obscuring the opening. In the small village, the hole remained a secret, although occasional rumours spread as to what might lie below ground.

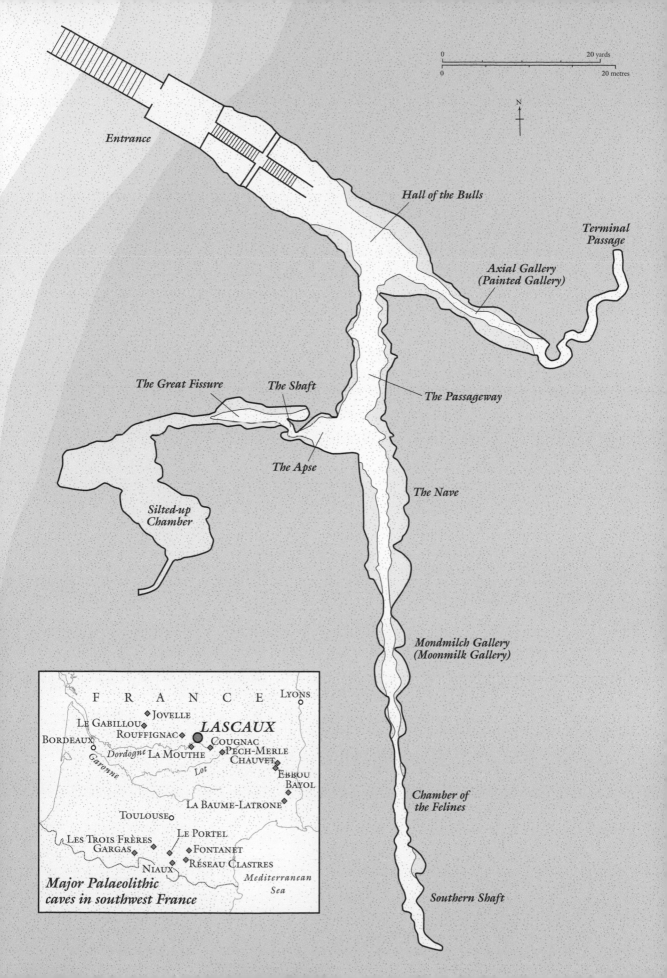

0   20 yards

0   20 metres

N

Entrance

Hall of the Bulls

Terminal Passage

Axial Gallery (Painted Gallery)

The Great Fissure

The Shaft

The Passageway

The Apse

Silted-up Chamber

The Nave

Mondmilch Gallery (Moonmilk Gallery)

Chamber of the Felines

Southern Shaft

F R A N C E

LYONS

◆ JOVELLE

LE GABILLOU ◆
ROUFFIGNAC ◆

LASCAUX

BORDEAUX
Dordogne LA MOUTHE ◆
Garonne

◆ COUGNAC
◆ PECH-MERLE
CHAUVET ◆

Lot

◆ EBBOU
BAYOL

LA BAUME-LATRONE ◆

TOULOUSE ○

LE PORTEL ◆

LES TROIS FRÈRES ◆
GARGAS ◆

◆ FONTANET

NIAUX ◆
◆ RÉSEAU CLASTRES

Mediterranean Sea

Major Palaeolithic caves in southwest France

Although much of France was under German occupation during the Second World War, Montignac remained in the free zone. In September 1940, four bored adolescents were looking for something to do, headed by one Marcel Ravidat, a seventeen-year-old apprentice garage mechanic and his dog, Robot. No doubt fuelled by the rumours about what lay beneath the ground at Lascaux, and intrigued by the thought of illicitly stashed treasure, the boys went to inspect the hole. As they did so, Robot swiftly disappeared inside it. Using penknives to widen the opening, the boys succeed in rescuing the dog, and discovered the carcass of a donkey that had clearly become trapped and died. A few days later, Ravidat returned with another group of friends, this time armed with better digging equipment, some lengths of rope and a lamp fashioned from an old oil pump. Having dug open the entrance, Ravidat was lowered into the hole on a rope. Following an unsteady descent, he found himself on the floor of a subterranean cavern. Wandering into a neighbouring passageway, he held his lamp up in front of him and saw, in the flickering light, that the wall was covered with astonishing drawings of animals. The teenager had accidentally stumbled upon one the world's finest collections of prehistoric cave paintings, hailed as the Sistine Chapel of prehistory by Abbé Breuil, a Catholic priest and the first expert to examine the

cave. Its walls were daubed with numerous well-preserved images – brilliantly realised and created using a wide variety of pigments – of aurochs, ibex, musk ox, European bison, a reindeer, rhinoceros and lions.

News of the find attracted scholars and the curious from far and wide. Once the war was over, the people of Montignac were keen to show their cave to the world. It wasn't too long, however, before patches of green mould began to appear on the cave walls. The cause was traced to pollen and other microorganisms carried in on the mud on visitors' shoes. To prevent any further damage, the cave was closed to the public for good in 1963. Twenty years later, in 1983, Lascaux II opened on the same hill – a facsimile of part of the cave, moulded in concrete and painted as closely to the original as possible, based on extensive photographs. This ersatz version attracted over ten million visitors and became a beloved national monument in its own right. In 2016, and at cost of fifty-seven million euros, it was supplanted by Lascaux IV, the International Centre for Cave Art, at the foot of the hill. Featuring an impressive three-dimensional, digitally rendered replica of the grotto that Ravidat and Robot found seventy-six years earlier, it – like those hybrid vines – allows ancient French art to live on without fear of further deterioration.

ABOVE: The paintings at Lascaux date from 16,000–14,000 BC. The Hall of Bulls features stags, horses and four bulls, all seemingly in motion.

39° 39' 30.5" N 113° 42' 42.4" E

XUANKONG SI

CHINA

Shanxi Province

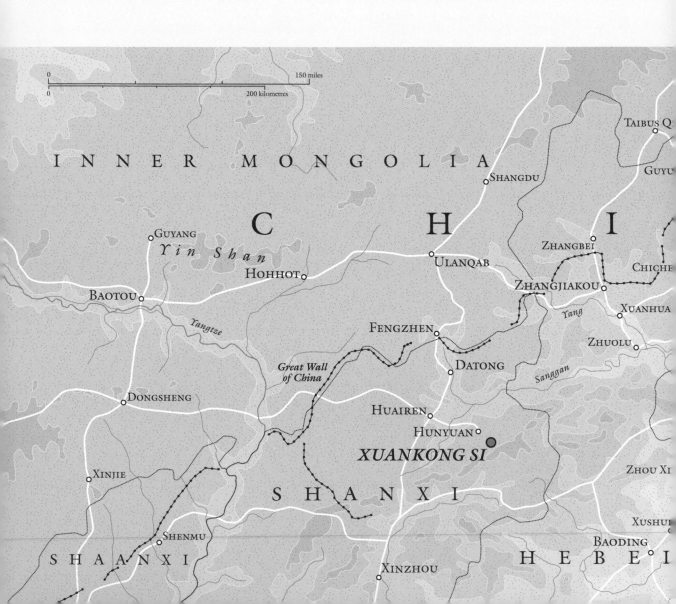

0   150 miles

0   200 kilometres

INNER MONGOLIA

TAIBUS Q

SHANGDU

GUYU

C   H   I

GUYANG

Yin Shan

ZHANGBEI

HOHHOT

ULANQAB

CHICHE

ZHANGJIAKOU

BAOTOU

Yangtze

Yang

XUANHUA

FENGZHEN

ZHUOLU

*Great Wall
of China*

DATONG

Sanggan

DONGSHENG

HUAIREN

HUNYUAN

ZHOU XI

XUANKONG SI

XINJIE

S   H   A   N   X   I

XUSHUI

SHENMU

BAODING

SHAANXI

XINZHOU

H   E   B   E   I

In many of the world's religions, godliness is associated with great height, and the mountain motif is not uncommon. In the Hindu tradition, for example, the Himalayas are not simply a range of majestic snow-capped peaks on the south Asian horizon, they are the abode of gods; Mount Olympus played a similar role for the ancient Greeks. Buddhists, Hindus, Christians and some Muslims revere Sri Pada, in Sri Lanka, as a holy mountain; depending on the creed, Buddha, Shiva or Adam scaled its slopes, supposedly leaving hefty footprints at its peak. According to the Judeo-Christian Bible, Moses communed with God, who presented him with the Ten Commandments, on Mount Sinai.

Associations with the sky above our heads and the celestial run even deeper. In the ancient indigenous Chinese tian religion, for example, the word *tian* – meaning a 'supreme power that rules over lesser Gods and all human life' – translates as heaven or sky. Traditionally, the Chinese referred to their rulers as the sons of heaven or *tianzi*, with their authority emanating directly from tian. Some Taoists meanwhile, believe that the ancient Chinese philosopher, Lao Tzu, himself ascended into the sky, to become an immortal in what they knew as the celestial High Pure Realm.

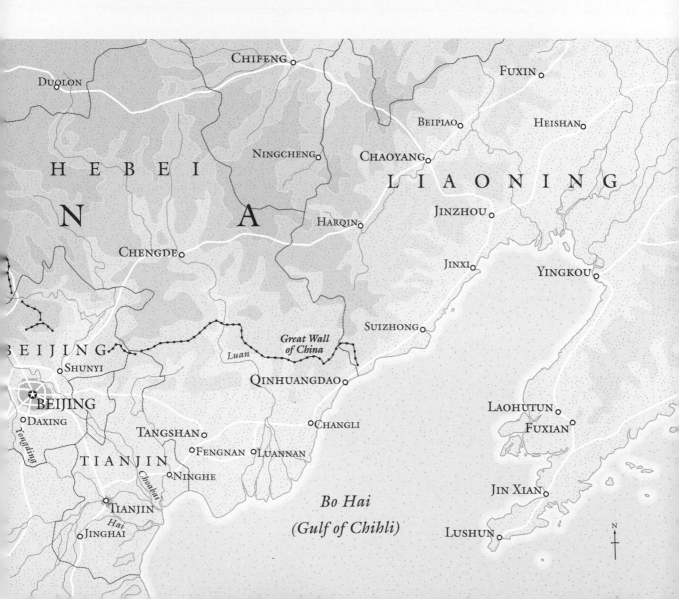

According to legend, Taoist builders came to the aid of Liao Ran, a Chinese monk living towards the end of the Northern Wei dynasty, in helping to construct a temple monastery that aimed to get closer to that High Pure Realm. A head for heights is required with a visit to Xuankong Si (the Hanging Temple), which is fixed to the cliff face of Mount Heng in Shanxi province, some 75 m (246 ft) aboveground. You also need a degree of faith in the engineering, because it is not immediately obvious how it is fixed. The cluster of dinky pagodas with their slatted wooden walkways is apparently held in place by a set of oak beams that, much like dowels on flat-pack shelving, are simply slotted into holes chiselled into the rockface. It hardly inspires confidence in stability: the splintering of a plank or two and the whole thing could seemingly tumble down the mountainside. Yet this temple has rested here, without coming to harm, for more than 1,400 years; the last major round of repairs took place in 1900. It has been suggested that the main body of the structure actually rests on bedrock and its position, slightly canopied by an overhanging chunk of cliff, offers protection from the elements and inclement weather.

Aside from its seemingly precarious, acrophobia-inducing locality, Xuankong Si is the only remaining temple in the country to be dedicated to China's three principle religions, Buddhism, Confucianism and Taoism – statues of the three founding figures, Buddha, Confucius and Lao Tzu are enshrined together in the temple's San Jiao Hall. One possible reason given for this multiplicity of faiths, is that the place was once a rare stopping-off point for travellers in the region. As such it welcomed weary wayfarers of all religions, attending to their spiritual, as well as physical, needs.

RIGHT: Within the temple complex are forty rooms connected by a series of corridors, bridges and walkways, and housing some eighty statues of bronze, iron and clay.

MATMATA VILLAGE
Tunisia
Matmata

Dream holidays are often said to be out of this world. In a sense, all holidays take us away from our known worlds – not matter how exotic (or not) the destination – and present a chance to experience something other than the familiar, the quotidian and the humdrum. Until very recently, the idea of holidaying in outer space was the stuff of science fiction, but leaving Earth's orbit is not entirely out the question these days. Richard Branson's Virgin Galactic, Elon Musk's SpaceX and Blue Origin from Amazon founder Jeff Bezos are all on the brink of offering tourist trips into space. The downside for the moment, however, is the price – just as it was in the early days of aviation – and with fares expected to run into the millions, only the super-wealthy will be booking flights any time soon. To compensate, however, there is a place on Earth that looks a little like outer space – or another planet, to be precise – a place that is familiar to the millions of viewers of the Star Wars movie franchise.

Matmata is a small village in southern Tunisia with a population of just over 2,000, some 40 km (25 miles) to the southwest of Gabès, the old coastal city on the Mediterranean that serves as the last point of entry or departure to the arid hills of the Sahara desert. In 1976, George Lucas and the cast and crew of the first Star Wars film came to Matmata and immortalised its dusty landscape, casting its Berber buildings as desert dwellings on the planet Tatooine – a world blessed with two moons but still derided in the film by Luke Skywalker as a place 'farthest from' the 'bright centre to the universe'.

Situated on a shelf of soft sandstone, the village of Matmata lies next to the only traversable land path between Libya and Tunisia. The Berbers have dug out homes in this region for centuries – cave dwellings of this type are believed to date back to the fourth century BC, although Matmata itself was largely settled in the sixteenth or seventeenth

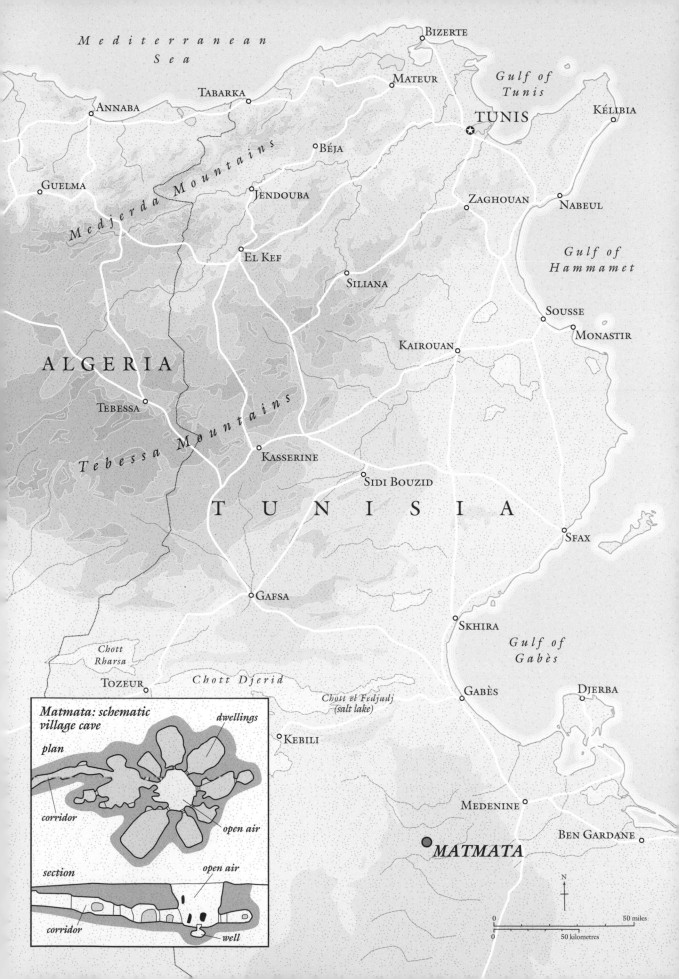

Mediterranean
Sea

BIZERTE

ANNABA   TABARKA   MATEUR   KÉLIBIA

Gulf of
Tunis

BÉJA   ★ TUNIS

GUELMA   ZAGHOUAN   NABEUL

Medjerda Mountains   JENDOUBA

EL KEF   Gulf of
Hammamet

SILIANA

SOUSSE

ALGERIA   KAIROUAN   MONASTIR

TEBESSA

Tebessa Mountains   KASSERINE

SIDI BOUZID   TUNISIA

SFAX

GAFSA

SKHIRA

Chott
Rharsa   Gulf of
Gabès

Chott Djerid

Chott el Fedjudj
(salt lake)   GABÈS   DJERBA

TOZEUR

KEBILI

MEDENINE

● MATMATA   BEN GARDANE

Matmata: schematic village cave

plan

dwellings

corridor   open air

section   open air

corridor   well

N

0   50 miles
0   50 kilometres

century. Although the original inhabitants of North Africa, Berbers make up only one per cent of the Tunisian population today, and frequently suffer discrimination as an ethnic minority. Their underground settlements, with subterranean housing and walkways, initially offered refuge from the subsequent waves of invaders and other rival tribal predators, but also from the heat of the daytime sun and the chill of the desert evenings.

The dwellings are formed around a central pit or courtyard, and were traditionally carved out of the malleable sandstone using hand tools.

One such Berber structure in Matmata appeared in *Star Wars*, later subtitled *Episode IV: A New Hope*, as the home of Luke Skywalker and his Uncle Owen and Aunt Beru Lars. By then, and since 1969 in fact, this particular building had been welcoming visitors as the hotel Sidi Driss, and is open to tourists today, who have flocked here in increasingly large numbers since the Star Wars franchise was rebooted in the late 1990s.

Many Berber people continue to make their homes in these underground dwellings. However, since the creation in the late 1950s, of Nouvelle Matmata, a new town with more conventional houses about 15 km (9 miles) up the road to Gabès, the numbers of those choosing to live below ground has been dwindling constantly.

RIGHT: The original Berber dwellings housed up to three generations of one family. Today, a number of them form a Berber museum (top). Pictured below is the *Star Wars* set at Hotel Sidi Driss.

SHELL GROTTO
ENGLAND
Margate, Kent

It was during the eighteenth century that former seaside fishing villages, such as Margate, on Britain's Kentish coast, first began to attract the affluent – even aristocratic – unwell, who came to avail themselves of the briny sea water, at the time proscribed as a curative to such ailments as gout. The establishment of the Royal Sea Bathing Hospital in 1791 saw the town become the country's most fashionable marine watering place in the country; its only serious rival at that time was Scarborough in North Yorkshire. But with the arrival of Cockney trippers from London, on boats on the Thames called hoys, Margate slowly shed its stuffily genteel image to become the first coastal resort to cater for the working classes.

'There is', the popular novelist and mystic Marie Corelli would write close to a century later, in 1885, 'something not exactly high-class in the name of Margate. Sixpenny teas are suggested, and a vulgar flavour of shrimps floats unbidden in the air.' But Corelli was fascinated by one particular attraction of the resort – one that, had it not been in 'plebeian Margate', she believed would 'be acknowledged as one of the wonders of the world'. That attraction was the Shell Grotto.

As a subsequent guidebook would put it, 'an air of mystery hangs over this remarkable excavation' and indeed one of the most recent volumes exploring its much disputed history is tellingly entitled *The Enigma of the Margate Shell Grotto*. Even the attraction's own official website simply claims: 'We don't know!' as a standard response to many of the questions posed by the public about the grotto's history and creation.

The facts, such as they are, run something like this: during the construction of a washhouse for a girls' school run by a Mr Newlove in 1834 (or 1835 or 1837, depending on your source), a workman cast aside a shovel only to find it disappear through a hole in the ground. A boy was duly dispatched to recover the shovel. Lowered down into the hole, the child encountered a cavern whose walls and central column were decorated with an array of shells, some twenty-eight varieties in all and the majority of local origin, all arranged into elaborate designs of sunflowers, lilies, clustered grapes, palm branches and serpent's heads.

Subsequent investigations would uncover a much-trumpeted 'two thousand square feet of shell-work' (186 m²). This artistry has ever since been alternately attributed to the Romans, followers of the Persian sun god cult of Mithras, bored late-eighteenth-century artisans, and fraudulent seaside speculators. Whatever its precedents, the cavern's decorations suffered from souvenir hunters chipping shells off the walls, the after effects of smoke from gas illuminations, and damp resulting from poor drainage caused by the ill-considered concreting aboveground. In 1999, the grotto was placed on the English Heritage Buildings at Risk Register, and extensive conservation work has been undertaken on the attraction since that time. Concurrently, this notoriously faded of seaside towns has itself enjoyed something of a new lease of life with the opening of the Turner Contemporary art gallery and the reopening of Margate's once cherished Dreamland amusement park. The grotto, meanwhile, with its rather charmingly tarnished shells, enchants precisely because it remains a slightly decayed oddity whose origins continue to be obscure, even historically dubious, and are all the more captivating for it.

ABOVE: Every surface of the cavernous grotto in Margate has been painstakingly inlaid with shells in intricate, often symmetrical, patterns.

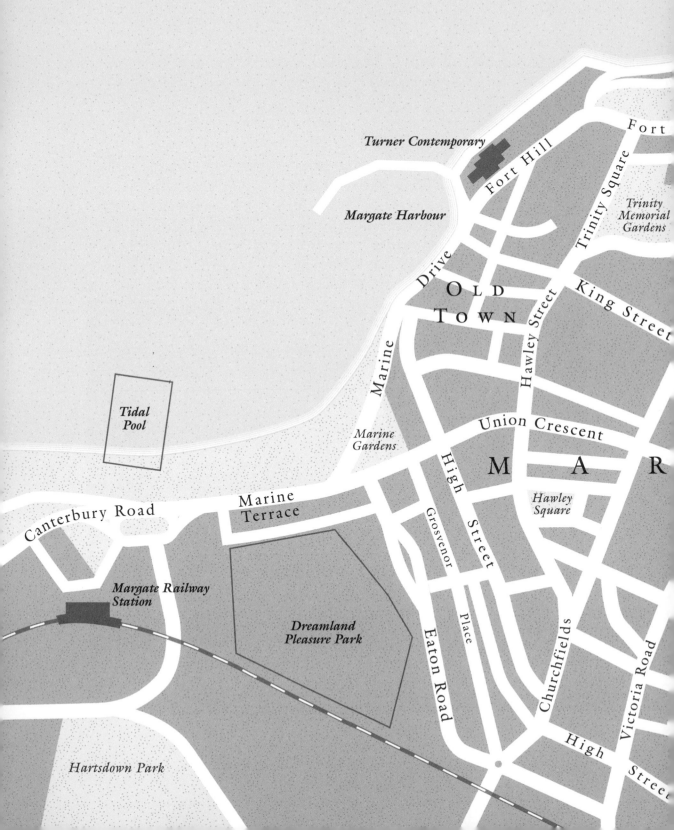

NORTH SEA

Turner Contemporary

Fort Hill

Fort

Trinity Square

Trinity Memorial Gardens

Margate Harbour

Drive

Marine

OLD TOWN

Hawley Street

King Street

Union Crescent

Marine Gardens

MAR

Tidal Pool

Hawley Square

Marine Terrace

High Street

Canterbury Road

Grosvenor Place

Street

Margate Railway Station

Dreamland Pleasure Park

Churchfields

Victoria Road

Eaton Road

High Street

Hartsdown Park

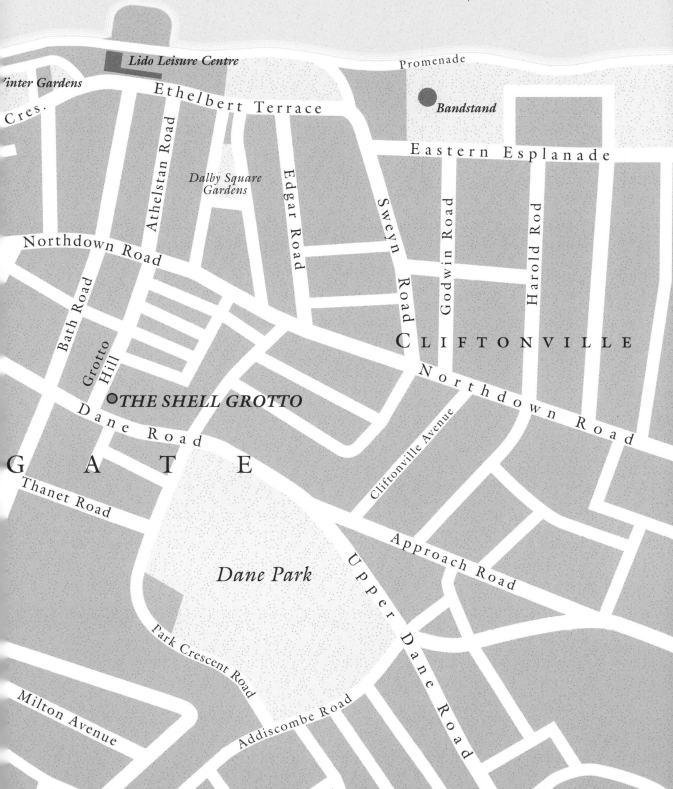

400 yards
0
400 metres

N

Lido Leisure Centre

Winter Gardens

Promenade

Cres.

Ethelbert Terrace

Bandstand

Eastern Esplanade

Dalby Square Gardens

Athelstan Road

Edgar Road

Sweyn Road

Godwin Road

Harold Rod

Northdown Road

CLIFTONVILLE

Bath Road

Grotto Hill

THE SHELL GROTTO

Northdown Road

Dane Road

GATE

Cliftonville Avenue

Thanet Road

Approach Road

Dane Park

Upper Dane Road

Milton Avenue

Park Crescent Road

Addiscombe Road

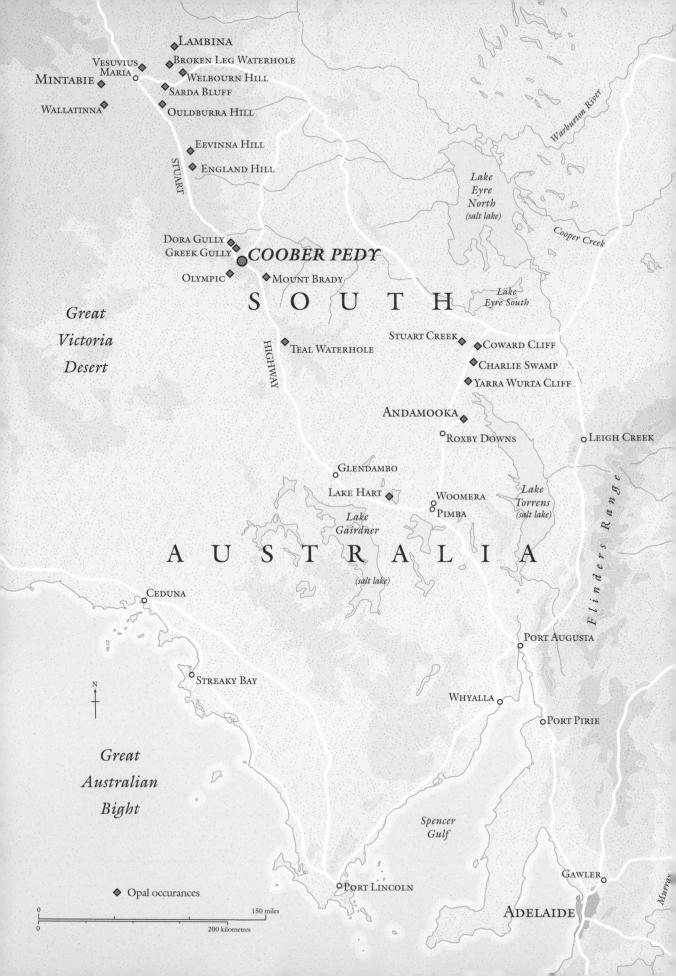

LAMBINA

VESUVIUS
MARIA
MINTABIE
BROKEN LEG WATERHOLE
WELBOURN HILL
SARDA BLUFF
WALLATINNA
OULDBURRA HILL

EEVINNA HILL
ENGLAND HILL

STUART

Warburton River

Lake
Eyre
North
(salt lake)

Cooper Creek

DORA GULLY
GREEK GULLY
COOBER PEDY
OLYMPIC
MOUNT BRADY

SOUTH

Lake
Eyre South

Great
Victoria
Desert

HIGHWAY

TEAL WATERHOLE

STUART CREEK
COWARD CLIFF
CHARLIE SWAMP
YARRA WURTA CLIFF

ANDAMOOKA
ROXBY DOWNS
LEIGH CREEK

Lake
Torrens
(salt lake)

Flinders Range

GLENDAMBO
LAKE HART
WOOMERA
PIMBA

Lake
Gairdner

AUSTRALIA

(salt lake)

CEDUNA

PORT AUGUSTA

STREAKY BAY

WHYALLA

PORT PIRIE

Great
Australian
Bight

N

Spencer
Gulf

GAWLER

Murray

◆ Opal occurances

PORT LINCOLN

ADELAIDE

0
150 miles
0
200 kilometres

COOBER PEDY

AUSTRALIA

South Australia

In 1851, the discovery of gold in New South Wales, Australia, brought prospectors to the country in their droves. The search for gold and other precious minerals continued well into the twentieth century, with miners enduring punishing conditions as they scoured the outback for potential spoils. In 1915, one band of prospectors had reached what might not unreasonably be called the middle of nowhere. Lying in South Australia in the southeastern corner of a desert the size of Germany and France combined, Coober Pedy is some long, and mostly exceedingly dry, 847 km (526 miles) from the beaches of Adelaide, the state's coastal capital. With temperatures exceeding 37°C (100°F) in the summer months, and little in the way of shade or rainfall to offset such heat, it is possibly one of the most inhospitable places on the planet. But this didn't deter our miners when staking it out, their heads filled with dreams of ingots and untold wealth; neither did it prevent Willie Hutchinson, a bored fourteen-year-old charged with minding the prospector's camp, from wandering off and stumbling upon some opals. The precious gemstones, there for young Willie's picking, sat just an inch or so below the sandstone ground that makes up this region's lunar-like landscape.

In light of Hutchinson's discovery, Coober Pedy exploded as an opal-mining town, its population swelling rapidly after the First World War, with many returning soldiers seeking to make their fortunes here rather than farm land under government-sponsored settlement schemes. Though riches were often only a day's dig away, that day was unvaryingly spent working under a punishingly hot sun and the evening that followed, bitterly cold. Seeking to ameliorate such extremes, the residents of Coober Pedy began to colonise the spent opal tunnels and exhausted mine shafts underground. Finding life below the surface, where conditions could be kept constant, infinitely preferable to the sun-scorched and desert-wind-

BELOW: Above the ground, all that can be seen of Coober Pedy are the raised mounds of waste rock brought up by the miners' drills (right). They betray nothing of the dwellings that exist below. In 1993, the community carved an underground church from the sandstone (left).

lashed surface, a whole new below-the-top-town sprang up, as people dug out bespoke dwellings and moved permanently underground.

Opals continue to be mined in Coober Pedy, which currently has a population of around 3,500 people. Some 80 per cent of those live in subterranean accommodation, much of it self-built and surprisingly homely too, despite the lack of natural light. Two supermarkets and a golf course are among the aboveground amenities of the town, but are put to shame by the plethora of sub-surface facilities, which include a church, a bookshop, a bar and a hotel. In any case, more than one century of mining has made the surface quite a treacherous territory. With a local desert terrain that is riddled with unmarked holes and open shafts, signs that warn against running and walking backwards, reinforce the feeling that the firmer ground is under the surface at Coober Pedy.

43° 49' 32.5" N, 28° 33' 38" E

MOVILE CAVE

ROMANIA

Constanța County

In his 1912 novel *The Lost World*, Sir Arthur Conan Doyle, creator of Sherlock Holmes and believer in fairies, charted, in boy's-own-adventure style with a slice of science fiction thrown in, an expedition to a distant plateau. On exploring the region, Professor Challenger and his companions encounter prehistoric dinosaurs, cannibalistic ape men and other species thought extinct elsewhere, all living atavistically on. If always to be overshadowed by his Baker Street stories, the book was a popular success. Doyle wrote four sequels featuring the character Professor Challenger, and it has been adapted for film and television many times. Doyle's remote landscape was purely fictional – his creatures the work of his vivid imagination. Were he seeking inspiration today, however, there is a corner of Romania that might easily have caught his fancy, a place in which fantastical life forms abound.

Not too far from Constanța, the 2,000-year-old port city on the Black Sea, in southeast Romania, there is a plain near Mangalia in Constanța County, that truly exemplifies the topographical formation – or lack of it. For, here, the region's featurelessness is so complete that it goes beyond qualifying as lowland or flatland, and becomes somewhat desolate and surreal in its utter barrenness. It is easy to understand why officials from communist Romania mooted the idea of building a power plant here. It is arguably one of those rare expanses of land on which the sight of any building might bring some form of relief. In 1986 engineers arrived here to test the ground for construction and, in doing so, they accidentally unearthed a most incredible lost world.

What the engineers had discovered while digging around was a labyrinth of subterranean caverns that had remained sealed for more than five million years. Their isolation has continued since being discovered, with fewer than one hundred people having descended the 20 m (66 ft) or so into the depths of what is now known as Movile Cave.

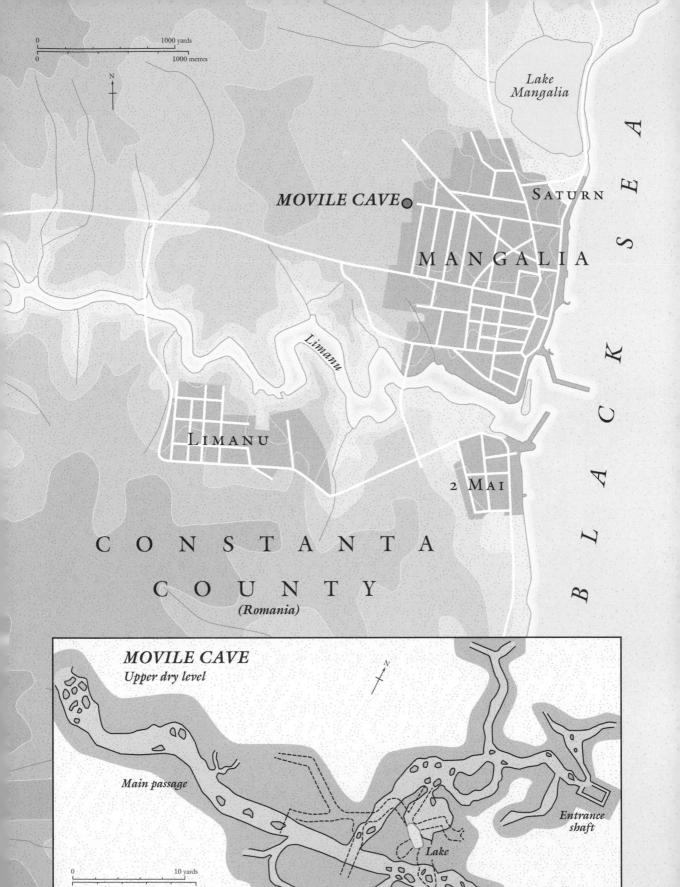

0   1000 yards

0   1000 metres

N

Lake Mangalia

MOVILE CAVE○

S A T U R N

M A N G A L I A

B L A C K   S E A

Limanu

L I M A N U

2 M A I

C O N S T A N T A

C O U N T Y

(Romania)

MOVILE CAVE
Upper dry level

N

Main passage

Lake

Entrance shaft

0   10 yards

0   10 metres

One reason for this is that the environment within this one-off ecosystem, at the bottom of which lies a lake of sulphidic water that reeks of rotting eggs, is decidedly hostile to humans. Containing around half the volume of oxygen as is normal in the air aboveground (10 per cent rather than 20 per cent), and around one hundred times the carbon dioxide, plus a percentage of hydrogen sulphide, the air is positively poisonous. Not only that, but it is dark – sunlight has been absent for millions of years. In spite of such conditions, and against all the odds, life of a unique sort has evolved and flourishes in this environment. So far forty-eight distinct species have been catalogued, thirty-three of which exist nowhere else on the planet. They consist mostly of spindly, blind and pigmentless creatures that crawl, slither and scuttle about – leeches, isopods, worms, spiders, shrimp and the like, with predominantly extended antennae and legs. That they live at all is nothing short of miracle. In the absence

of natural sunlight for photosynthesis, the cave offers one of Earth's few examples of an ecosystem that feeds purely off chemical reactions, with the bacteria at the base of the food chain converting the sulphides and ammonia in the cave's waters into organic compounds.

Odd as they are, the conditions in this cave could offer insight into the ways in which life first formed on Earth. When our world was in its primordial infancy, the sun's rays were blocked by a dense atmosphere of carbon dioxide, methane and ammonia. It is therefore possible that some of the planet's first creatures emerged from similarly unprepossessing circumstances and that Movile Cave offers a window into our own evolution.

BELOW: The plains country near Mangalia in Constanța County stretches for miles, with little in the way of relief, except a natural lake around which wild grasses grow.

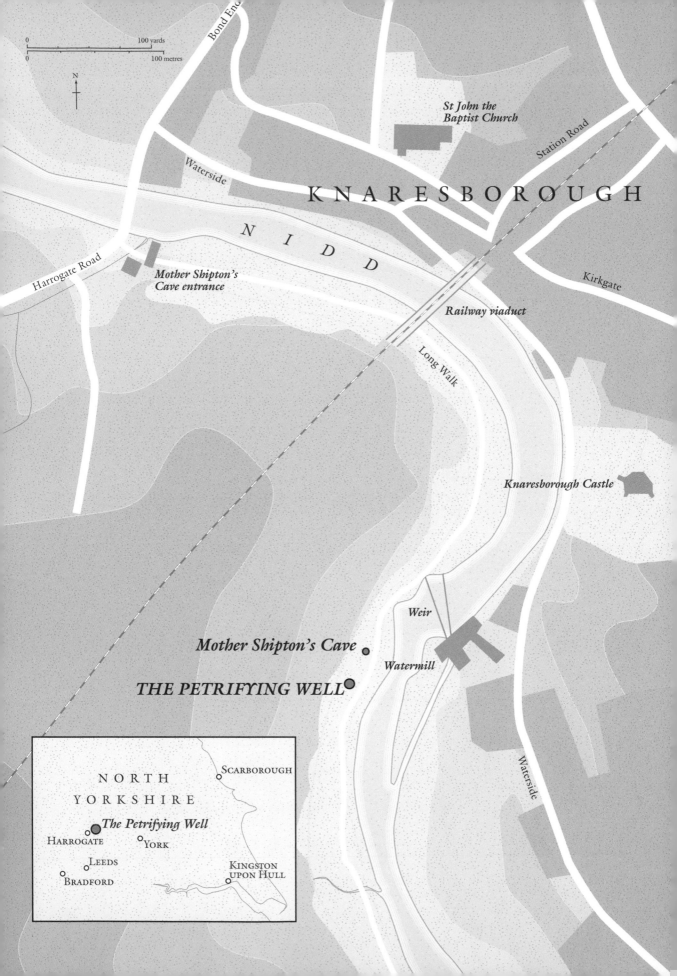

Bond End

100 yards
100 metres

0
0

N

Waterside

Harrogate Road

St John the
Baptist Church

Station Road

KNARESBOROUGH

N I D D

Mother Shipton's
Cave entrance

Kirkgate

Railway viaduct

Long Walk

Knaresborough Castle

Mother Shipton's Cave

Weir

THE PETRIFYING WELL

Watermill

Waterside

NORTH
YORKSHIRE

SCARBOROUGH

The Petrifying Well

HARROGATE

YORK

LEEDS

BRADFORD

KINGSTON
UPON HULL

54° 00' 31.3" N 1° 28' 29.3" W

THE PETRIFYING WELL

ENGLAND

Knaresborough, Yorkshire

Perched on the limestone cliffs above the Nidd River and the scenic Nidd Gorge, Knaresborough is a naturally stony sort of place. This august, North Yorkshire market town, located in the remnants of The Royal Forest of Knaresborough, is dominated by the ruined walls and keep of a fourteenth century royal castle that sits on the brow of its hill. Some of Knaresborough's oldest buildings were fashioned from stone salvaged from the castle, and its steepest alleys and walkways retain their ankle-twisting cobbles. Beyond the town lies the pleasure-garden-turned-nature-park, Plumpton Rocks – named after the dramatic Millstone Grit rock formations found there. Another of Knareborough's geologically tinged assets is a cave believed to have been the birthplace of Old Mother Skipton. Local legend has it that this crone-like Tudor prophetess predicted the death of Mary, Queen of Scots. She is also said to have had a way with magical healing herbs from the nearby forest. Open to the public since 1630, the cave claims to be Britain's oldest tourist attraction and under the stewardship of the Slingsby family – the local aristocratic landowners – the site became a popular destination for the sightseeing gentry of Georgian and Victorian England. Adjoining the cave was an additional feature that drew them to the area; Skipton's Petrifying Well, once known as the Dropping Well, and believed by some to be cursed by the devil.

The peculiar qualities of this natural water feature were first recorded by John Leland, the poet and chaplain, librarian and antiquary to King Henry VIII. After visiting Knaresborough in 1538, he wrote of 'a Welle of wonderful nature' whose waters turned whatever was cast into them into stone. Despite having this alarming effect on inanimate objects, its waters were prized as a curative and many drank it or bathed in it to see off 'any flux of the body'.

Fortunately, medical science has progressed, and physicians warn strongly against such activities today, particularly against ingesting the water. Modern chemical analysis has shown that the well's water contains an unusually high concentration of calcite, a mineral derived from the surrounding tufa and travertine rock through which the water passes. It is also the high level of calcite that gives the water special power to petrify. As such, it transforms almost anything left in its path into stone within a matter of months. A top hat and bonnet left in the flow of the well's waters in 1853 have now assumed forms close to boulders and are all but unrecognisable.

Among the more interesting and recognisable items that can be inspected in the well's museum today, is a petrified handbag left by Britain's famed crime writer, Agatha Christie, a hat once worn by the big-screen cowboy John Wayne and a shoe deposited by Queen Mary when she visited the well in 1923. Curiously, teddy bears and soft toys are among the most popular items dunked into the mineralising streams of this well, and suitably transmogrified bears are sold as souvenirs in the attraction's gift shop.

For those who find petrification and devil's curses a little creepy, there is also an ancient wishing well nearby, believed to grant good fortune to those who cast a coin into its waters. For those who don't want their luck to run out too soon, or wish to take their chances with them, bottles of the water can be purchased.

RIGHT: Among the many teddy bears suspended in the well's constant flow are a mask, a floppy hat and a lobster. Other petrifying objects include a top hat, a cricket bat and a stovetop kettle.

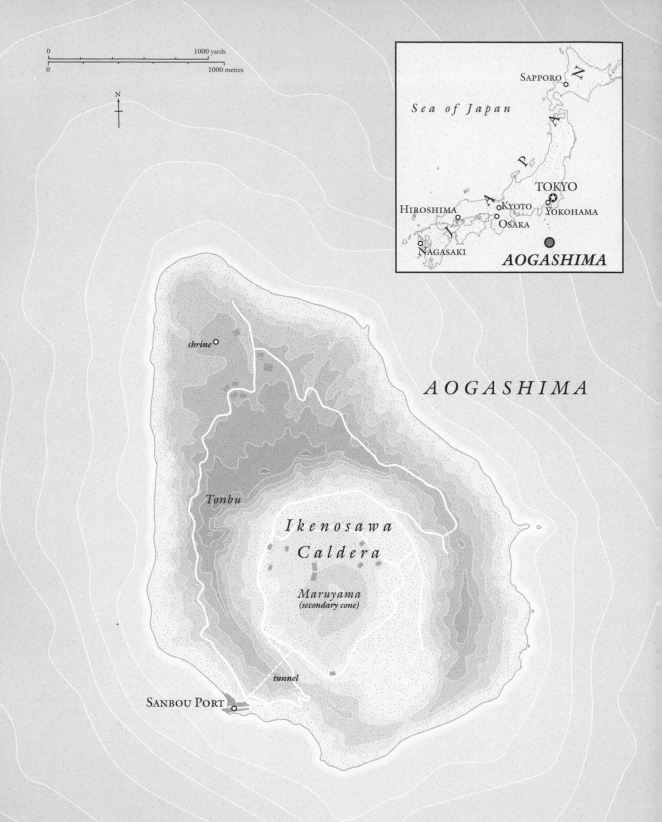

0 — 1000 yards
0 — 1000 metres

N

shrine ○

AOGASHIMA

Tonbu

Ikenosawa Caldera

Maruyama
(secondary cone)

tunnel

SANBOU PORT ○

PHILIPPINE SEA

Sea of Japan

SAPPORO

J A P A N

TOKYO

HIROSHIMA

KYOTO

YOKOHAMA

Osaka

NAGASAKI

AOGASHIMA

AOGASHIMA

Japan

Philippine Sea

When people talk about Aogashima, the Japanese island 320 km (200 miles) south of Tokyo in the Kuroshio region of the Philippine Sea, words beginning with the letter 's' tend to dominate. The island itself is postage-stamp-sized, a mere 3.5 km (2 miles) long and only 2.5 km (1.5 miles) wide. Its population is small, too, and has been shrinking. If technically made up of two hamlets, Yasundogo and Nishigo, Aogashima enjoys the status of the smallest village in Japan, with just 206 residents. Solitude is something inhabitants claim to value most of all about their island home, if pressed on the issue – that, and its serenity, along with acres of lush greenery. With one of the island businesses being a distillery, there is no shortage of shōchū, either – not dissimilar to vodka, shōchū is the national spirit of Japan and made from the sweet potatoes that, along with tomatoes and other vegetables, flourish in Aogashima's mineral-rich soil. A few shops and a salt works are among the other enterprises here, but in sharp contrast to the bustle of Tokyo, sleepiness reigns supreme here.

The greatest excitement arguably lies in getting on and off Aogashima in the first place, which is difficult – daring, even. Until 1993, when a daily helicopter service was introduced, the island was accessible only by boat. But the surrounding sea is notoriously rough and the island is constantly subjected to tropical storms and bathed in fog. Visitors have to accept the likelihood of being stranded for several days beyond their allotted stay. The chief attractions to outsiders are the peace and quiet, the scenery and the natural hot spring that lies slap bang in the middle of Aogashima. Its toasty geothermally heated waters power public showers, baths and a sauna, while its excess steam is funnelled out to a facility to cook fish and vegetables. Steamed dishes are, unsurprisingly, the island's culinary speciality. Steam is not confined to the spring, either. It spurts out of the ground in rocky craters here and there – a subtle reminder that Aogashima isn't an island as such, but the top half of an active volcano. Residents seem completely sanguine about any risks posed by living where they do. To some extent they have to be. Much of the main village lies on the outside of the volcano cone and, if it blew, nothing would survive. One of the earliest records of an eruption dates from 1652, while the last major eruption occured in the Endo period, in the summer of 1785, with devastating results. Almost half of the island's 327-strong population perished, as the volcano shot giant plumes of gas, smoke and burning rocks into the air. In the wake of such appalling devastation, the island remained uninhabited for the next fifty years or so, after which settlers gradually began to return. These days, the Japanese Meteorological Agency use the latest seismographic equipment to keep a constant tab on the volcano's activities.

For the time being, the inhabitants' trust in science to offer them advance warning, coupled with a will to stay on this quiet little island, appears to trump any fears of another sudden, ferocious eruption happening.

Another boon of the island is its lack of light pollution. The rake of its northern shore, entirely free of houses and street lights, is known as 'The Coliseum of the Stars' for the uninhibited views it provides of the heavens above. Perhaps living under such a canopy only adds to the islanders' sanguinity at their potentially impermanent place in the universe. The night sky is, after all, lit by stars as they once were, some long since gone, and their luminescence is a mere flickering trace of their past only just reaching our present.

BELOW: With steep, rocky cliffs covered in rich vegetation, Aogashima is made up from the remnants of four ancient calderas. The largest caldera, Ikenosawa, remains a dominant feature of the island.

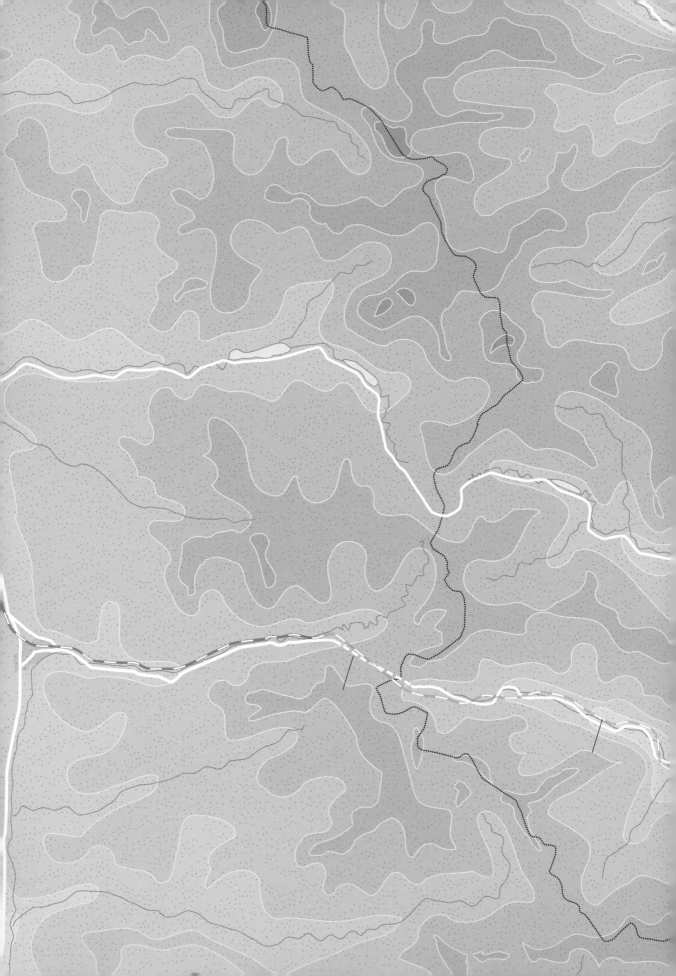

SERENDIPITOUS
SPACES

ZHANGYE DANXIA LANDFORM

CHINA

Gansu

Try not to go when it's damp and raining, advises one travel guide to the 'Rainbow Mountains' of Zhangye Danxia National Geopark, some 40 km (25 miles) west of the city of Zhangye, in China's Gansu province, once a starting-off point for the Silk Route. It is a tip, perhaps, worth heeding for many an outdoor attraction, where shelter could be sparse and the mildest drizzle, even in the most outstanding of locations, can put rather a damper on enjoying the surroundings. The great essayist and radical William Hazlitt once stated a preference for sundials over mechanical clocks on the grounds that they refused to tell the time in inclement weather. Similarly there are certain places in the world that just don't work without sunshine, and the Zhangye Danxia Landform may well be considered one of these. Visually, it is certainly at it best when the sun is out. Or at dawn and dusk, when the sunlight, waxing or waning, plays with the multitude of colours in this kaleidoscopic geological wonder. Yet without the damp and the rain, and the wind, there wouldn't really be a Zhangye Danxia worth visiting at all, for it is the weather and weathering that have made this landform what it is.

This is a story that begins millions and millions of years ago, when mineral-rich deposits of sandstone and siltstone began to build up, rising layer upon layer like the tiers of a cake, on the seabed of an ancient ocean. This tidy stratified arrangement was upended with the collision of the Indian and Eurasian plates around fifty-five million years ago, a tectonic event that formed the Himalayas. Here, the flat horizontal layers of sandstone were pushed up into the air as mountains, rather like a giant ruck in a carpet. This new undulating landscape exposed portions of sedimentary rock that previously would have remained buried underground to the elements. Those elements – whipping desert winds, driving rains and winter frosts – now had some raw material they could go to town on. The resulting range

of fantastical peaks and troughs, ridges and jutting outcrops is the product of persistent precipitation and erosion at its most artful. The polychromatic hues of yellows, oranges, reds, greens and blues that lend the range its psychedelic quality, stem from the oxidation of the variety of iron ores and minerals in the red sandstone from which it is formed. The term 'danxia' refers specifically to this type of landform and there are several other examples in this part of China, but none are quite so eye-catching or as colourful as Zhangye Danxia.

ABOVE: The Zhange Danxia Landform covers around 520 km² (200 sq miles) of Chinese territory. The alternating bands of coloured rock are its most striking feature.

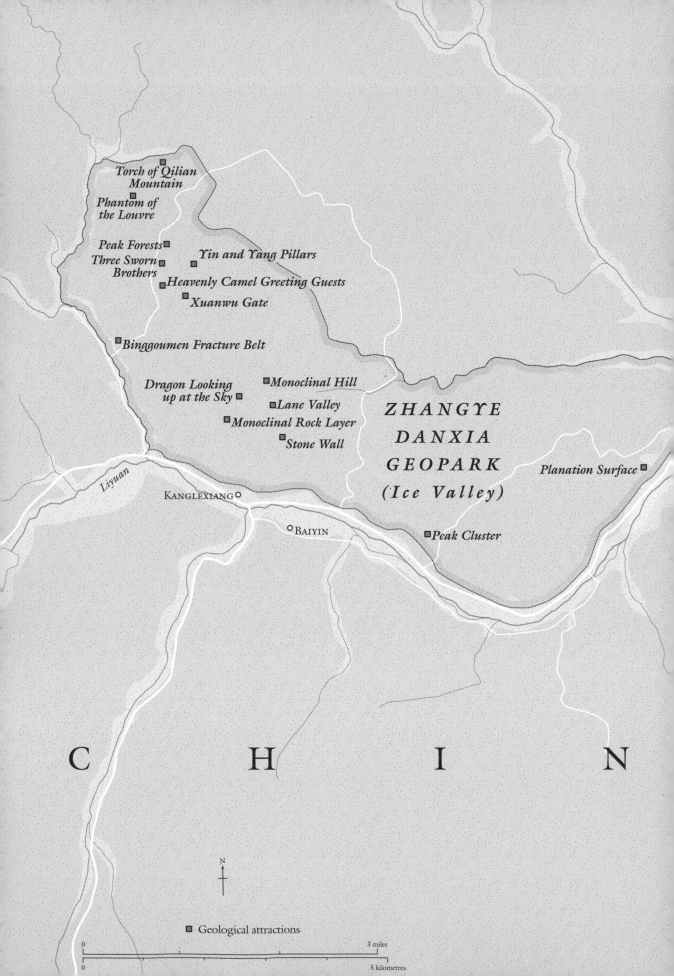

Torch of Qilian
Mountain

Phantom of
the Louvre

Peak Forests
Three Sworn
Brothers

Yin and Yang Pillars

Heavenly Camel Greeting Guests

Xuanwu Gate

Binggoumen Fracture Belt

Dragon Looking
up at the Sky

Monoclinal Hill

Lane Valley

Monoclinal Rock Layer

Stone Wall

ZHANGYE
DANXIA
GEOPARK
(Ice Valley)

Planation Surface

Liyuan

KANGLEXIANG

BAIYIN

Peak Cluster

C   H   I   N

N

■ Geological attractions

0   3 miles

0   5 kilometres

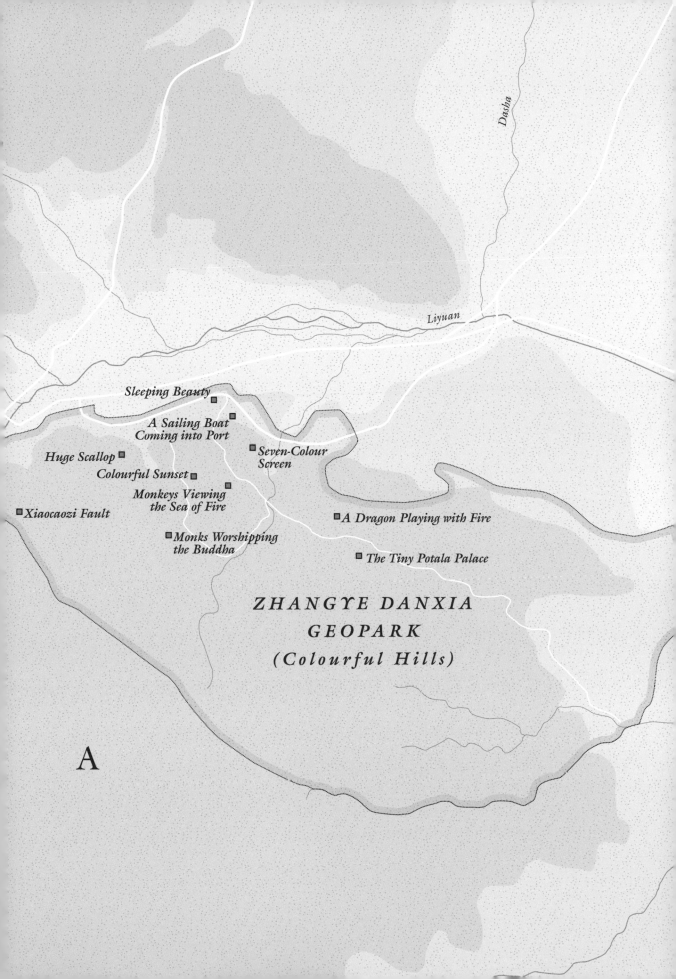

Dasha

Liyuan

Sleeping Beauty

A Sailing Boat
Coming into Port

Huge Scallop

Seven-Colour
Screen

Colourful Sunset

Monkeys Viewing
the Sea of Fire

Xiaocaozi Fault

A Dragon Playing with Fire

Monks Worshipping
the Buddha

The Tiny Potala Palace

ZHANGYE DANXIA
GEOPARK
(Colourful Hills)

A

46° 40' 31.5" S 169° 00' 07.0" E

SLOPE POINT
New Zealand
South Island

In a brief poem entitled 'Who Has Seen the Wind?', the English poet Christina Rossetti puts her finger on the fact that, while we can hear and feel the gentlest of breezes, we can only really observe winds indirectly from their effects on other things. As she writes:

> Who has seen the wind?
> Neither I nor you:
> But when the leaves hang trembling,
> The wind is passing through.

Wind is just moving air, its motion caused by changes in atmospheric pressure. That the air all around us appears transparent is the result of our retinas developing to detect the wavelengths of light that, if helpfully coming up short when faced with solids and liquids, pass right through the molecules of such gases as nitrogen, oxygen, argon, and carbon dioxide that make up our atmosphere. There are occasions when we seem to catch a glimpse of the air – when it's foggy, or there's a rainbow, say. However, we are merely observing the light interact with other particles – it's the water vapour in the air, for instance, that allows us to see the funnel of a raging tornado.

At Slope Point in New Zealand, the winds certainly rage, and it is their sheer relentlessness that has supplied this corner of rocky coastline with a most arresting visual spectacle. Slope Point is the southernmost tip of New Zealand's South Island and can only be reached by a twenty-minute walk across a few acres of private farmland. Beyond it, there are some 4,803 km (2,984 miles) of largely open sea to the South Pole. With little inbetween to obscure the airstreams that blow in from Antarctica – aside from bobbing icebergs and

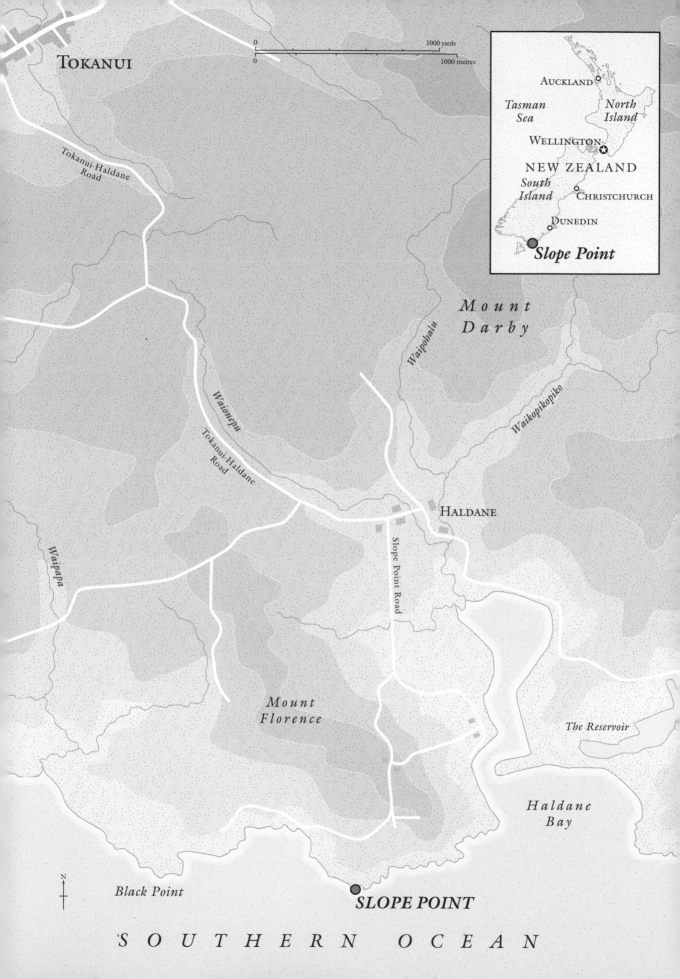

the odd seal's smooth head – Slope Point is constantly lashed by an icy southwesterly. Some days are less blustery than others, obviously, but at Slope Point every day is a gusty day, and unremittingly so for the most part. Pretty inhospitable for humans, the area's chief inhabitants are sheep, raised to graze on the mossy grass that abounds, despite the high winds. In some distant decade, or so the story goes, local farmers clubbed together to plant a few trees to provide shelter for their animals. They also erected a handful of rather pitiful shacks, remnants of which still stand. The trees flourished, but their trunks and branches grew twisted and warped from the constant battering of the winds blown in with the icy currents flowing in from the sea. Bent for so long by the whims of these winds, the trees at Slope Point today huddle together, their arched and outstretched fronds resembling follicles of hair caught mid blow-dry. As a living illustration of the power of the nature to shape the environment, the trees also, perhaps, offer the closest thing to ever seeing the wind. With practically only the end of the world in front of them, their forms lend a compellingly eerie aspect to the view.

ABOVE: The gnarled and warped trees at Slope Point provide the only relief in a windswept landscape that is primarily open pastureland leading to rocky cliffs.

39° 27' 02.9" N 123° 48' 46.6" W

GLASS BEACH

USA

Fort Bragg, California

On 18 April 1906, the San Francisco earthquake, and the fires that followed it, destroyed more than 28,000 buildings in the city and left over 3,000 people dead. The quake was not contained to the metropolitan area; it ruptured the San Andreas fault to the north and south for close to 480 km (300 miles). The effects of the quake were felt as far away as southern Oregon and inland to central Nevada. At Fort Bragg, a fishing and logging town on the Mendocino coast of the Pacific Ocean, in Northern California, all but two of its brick houses were laid waste by the earthquake.

In the immediate aftermath of the event, the streets of Fort Bragg were knee-deep in rubble. Looking to restore order as quickly as possible, the townspeople decided the most expedient solution was simply to push as much of the wreckage as possible over the edge of the cliffs and into the ocean. With the debris out of sight and out of mind, the business of putting the town back together again and felling and milling timber for the 'city by the bay' could start in earnest. It worked, too: Fort Bragg bounced back, bigger and better. Even today, the town's official website acknowledges that 'the earthquake brought prosperity to Fort Bragg' as its 'mills furnished lumber for the rebuilding of San Francisco.'

This new-found prosperity, however, brought problems of a different kind, since greater wealth and higher levels of consumption create more rubbish to be disposed of. Considering the success of the solution found in the wake of the earthquake, the people of Fort Bragg turned once more to their shore. It was not long before they were piling all kinds of rubbish – from old automobiles, broken appliances and furniture to tin cans and glass bottles – over the edge of the cliff. In time, their stretch of beach had become a festering tip referred to simply as 'The Dumps'.

PACIFIC OCEAN

Virgin Creek

Airport Road

GLASS BEACH

Pudding Creek Road

Bush   Street

Pudding Creek

Pine Street

Laurel Street

FORT BRAGG

Soldier Point

Oak Street

Main Street

Maple Street

Chestnut Street

Noyo Bay

NOYO

Noyo River

N

0	1000 yards
0	1000 metres

Once upon a time, this land had belonged to the Native American Pomo tribe, who knew it as Kah-Leh-deh-mun or 'the place surrounded by trees'. At that time this rocky shoreline had been shaded by a dense forest of pine trees and redwoods. There were oaks and buckeyes too, whose nuts and seeds the Pomo gathered to eat and grind into flour for making bread. From the forest floor they had harvested wild berries, greens and herbs, and through its trees darted after deer, rabbits and squirrels. And along this seashore they sought the bounty of the ocean, gathering kelp and catching fish with bone hooks. In stark contrast, all that stood here by the middle of the twentieth century was a mountain of rotting carburettors and rusting soup cans several feet high.

By the 1960s, and particularly in the aftermath of Rachel Carson's influential book, *Silent Spring* (1962), which drew attention to the harmful effects of pesticides and other pollutants, concerns were growing about the damage 'The Dumps' might be doing to the local environment. The regional water quality control board restricted what could be disposed of offshore and, in 1967, dumping at the beach was banned and a new landfill site established elsewhere. Some of the bulkier and more hazardous items were removed from the shore, but tonnes of material were left behind. The Pacific Ocean then began a clean-up operation of its own and, belying its name, set about thrashing this waste with its pounding waves, from low tide to high, and hour after hour.

Today, the beach at Fort Bragg glistens with thousands of sparkling, multicoloured glass stones, fragments from spent coke bottles and jam jars transformed into gems by the relentless churn of the sea. In their new shapes and sizes, these former rejects became so coveted by tourists and beachcombers that, in 2015, the local authorities – for fear of the shore being picked clean – made it illegal for anything to be taken from the beach. Officially part of the MacKerricher State Park, Glass Beach is one of Northern California's more unnaturally beautiful, natural beauty spots. Certain visitors come, like birders in search of rare breeds, to seek out particular fragments of ruby-red glass that hail from pre-1960s car taillights. From that time on, the automotive industry switched to plastic, a substance that continues to pose a terrible threat to our oceans and bedevil the environment.

LEFT: Thousands of fragments of glass, well worn by the sea, mingle with the pebbles on Glass Beach – a charming remnant of the beach's less glamorous past.

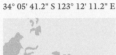

34° 05' 41.2" S 123° 12' 11.2" E

LAKE HILLIER

AUSTRALIA

Western Australia

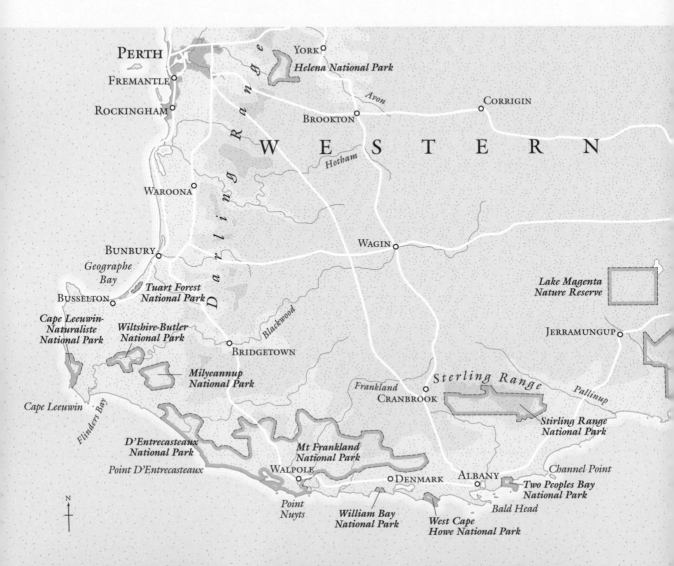

As lasting legacies go, the naming of a continent is not a bad one to chalk up for posterity. Admittedly Matthew Flinders, the Lincolnshire-born navigator, hydrographer, explorer and cartographer who gave us Australia, had the advantage of living between the end of the eighteenth and start of the nineteenth century, a period when the world's maps still contained a few gaps and the overall geographical grasp of certain territories remained shaky. (Not that these places were unknown to their native inhabitants, of course.) In 1801, as the commander of the 303-tonne (334-ton) HMS *Investigator*, Flinders was instructed by the British admiralty to embark on a voyage of exploration of southern Australia – at the time, referred to as 'the Unknown Coast'. Flinders' job was to ink in that unknown on paper, replacing what often amounted to wild speculation with solid topographic detail – detail that, in maps to come, would be tinged pink as a mark of its possession by the British empire. Flinders was good at his job and his charts continue to be consulted to this day.

Flinders was also the first European to circumnavigate Australia. It was while charting the country's coastline in January 1802 that he encountered and mapped a group of some one hundred islands, the Recherche Archipelago, off the southern shores of Western Australia.

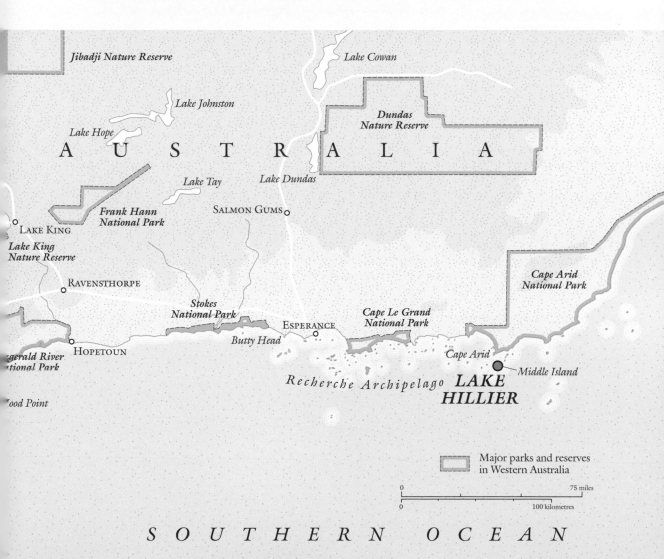

Flinders, his crew and the botanists aboard the ship spent a day or two exploring Middle Island, the largest of the archipelago. Seeking a bird's-eye view of the terrain to complete his survey, Flinders himself was to scale the island's highest hill, a 185 m (607 ft) mount now known as Flinders Peak. But it was Mr Thistle, the ship's master mariner, who reached a small lake on the northeastern part of the island that was 'of a rose colour' and saturated with salt; its pinkness was all the more striking because of the eucalyptus and other lush green vegetation around. Samples of its crystallised salt made a welcome addition to ship supplies. In tribute to an unfortunate member of the crew, one William Hillier, who had died of dysentery, they called it Lake Hillier.

The strawberry-milkshake colour of the lake is believed to derive from the particular cocktail of natural ingredients in the water, specifically *Dunaliella* algae, and high levels of mineral salts and sodium bicarbonate. Like Israel's Dead Sea, the salinity makes swimming in it almost impossible; bathers, however, can safely enjoy bobbing about on its surface. In the opening years of the twentieth century, salt was briefly mined from the lake, but the operation was abandoned six years later.

Flinders was to die in 1814, at just forty years of age and the day after the publication of his account of his voyages, *Terra Australis*. Within a decade, the title of this masterwork, and his coinage, had also been chosen as the name for the continent.

RIGHT: Surrounded by lush forest greenery and close by the Pacific Ocean, Lake Hillier measures just 600 m (1,970 feet) in length and is no more than 250 m (820 ft) wide.

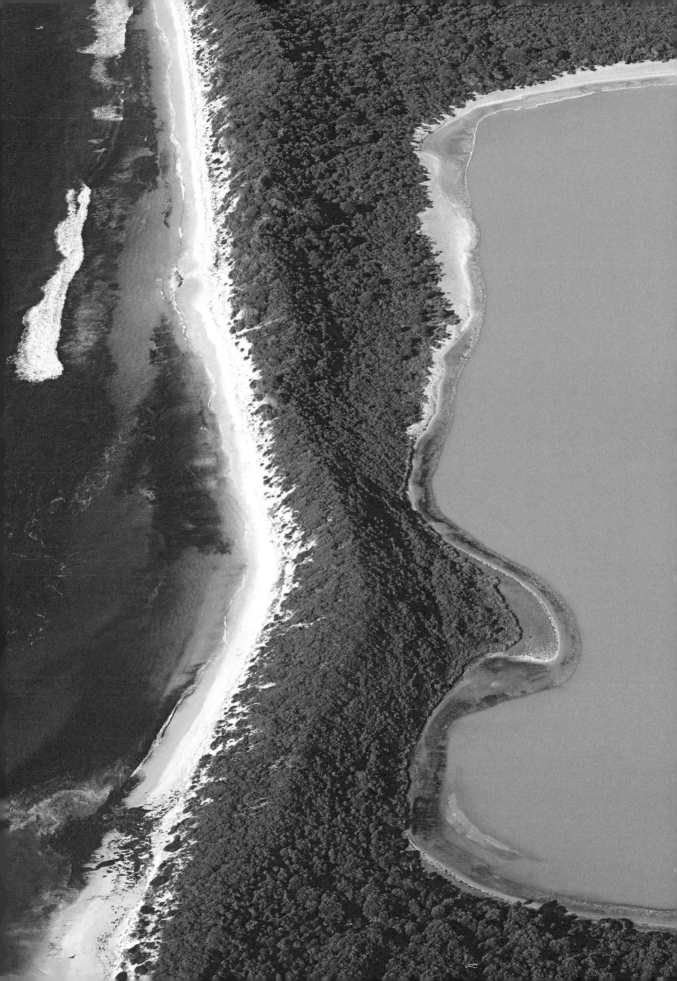

GRÜNER SEE

AUSTRIA

Styria

The etymological origins of the English word 'park' derive from the Old French *parc*, meaning 'an enclosed tract of land reserved for keeping and hunting deer and other game'. The roots of such hunting parks run deep. One of the earliest known descriptions of a park-type landscape appears in the epic of 'Gilgamesh'. This ancient Sumerian poem is believed to have been written in around 2000 BC, the text preserved on stone tablets from the Assyrian King Ashurbanipal's palace at Nineveh, near today's Mosul in Iraq. The poem tells the story of two friends: Gilgamesh, ruler of Uruk, one-third human and two-thirds deity; and Enkidu, a wild man of the woods previously given to consorting with animals. The story traces their quest to discover the secret of immortality. The search leads them to a sacred cedar forest, forbidden to mortals. Well tended, with winding trails and beautiful flowers, tall trees, sweet-smelling plants and exotic beasts, it is – to all intents and purposes – a park. It even has its own keeper, an ogre named Humbaba, whose breath is said to be 'like fire' and its jaws 'like death'.

Austria is some way from the Mesopotamia (modern day Iraq) of Gilgamesh but it is one of Europe's greenest countries. Almost half its landmass is covered in forest that once teemed with red deer that were hunted for game but that are now protected national parks. Styria, the central mountainous region, bills itself as 'the green heart of Austria' and boasts the Gesäuse National Park and is admired for its woods, meadows, grassland, orchards, vineyards – and one particularly pleasant country park. In the winter months, residents and visitors to the town of Tragöss in Stryia can avail themselves of this park. It lies beside a narrow and shallow lake known as the Grüner See, or Green Lake, at the foot of the snowcapped Hochschwab Mountains. As in almost every park in the world, there are footpaths, trees and wooden benches upon which to sit and survey the scene, rest legs weary

O B E R M   S E E

Maximum extent of lake

Minimum extent of lake

GRÜNER SEE

Julienheim

Protected

Area

G r u n a g e r

S c h a t t e n b e r g   S t r a ß e

Guesthouse

N

0   250 yards

0   250 metres

BELOW: Grüner See's striking emerald-green colour is attributed to the verdant foliage that grows during the winter months, but lies submerged in summer.

from hiking or, perhaps, indulge in an alfresco lunch of local spiced cheese on crisp black bread. Anyone returning to the area in spring or summer, however, will have to hunt high and low to find any trace of the park again. In its place, you would find a great expanse of crystal-clear emerald-green water. This is because the warmer weather causes the snow on the mountains to melt, swelling the lake and flooding the park in up to 12 m (40 ft) of water. Until banned in 2016, amid fears of pollution, the lake was a favourite destination for divers. They would swim among the park's benches and along its paths, all perfectly preserved, if eerily, completely submerged below the water, just like a miniature alpine Atlantis awaiting rediscovery.

PACIFIC OCEAN

TASHIROJIMA

ODOMARI

Odomari Dock

○ *Cat Shrine*

Nitoda Dock

NITODA

Totsura

N

| 0 | | 1000 yards |
| 0 | | 1000 metres |

CAT ISLAND

JAPAN

Tashirojima

D og lovers might argue that the whole notion of a domestic cat is an oxymoron, with felines exhibiting only the most perfunctory of commitments to their supposed owner's lives, while canine cohabitants of hearth and home can, by definition, be loyal to the point of doggedness. Recent scientific research would seem to indicate that cats effectively domesticated themselves.

The cat's journey from wild hunter to occupant of warm laps was closely tied to the development of farming in the Middle East. It was only with the establishment of grain stores, which attracted rodents, that cats began to venture into human settlements. Tolerated as efficient killers of pests, cats gradually started to inveigle their way into the emerging agricultural ecosystems of what is now Jordan, Syria and the region of Palestine in around 10–8000 BC. The cat's contribution was sufficiently valued in ancient Egypt, another significant cradle of agrarian civilisation, to become an object of religious veneration. It also led to cats being bred specifically for mummification and burial, to accompany wealthier Egyptians into their lavish graves and supposedly on into the afterlife.

Still, their usefulness as ratcatchers ensured their presence onboard the ships of Phoenician sailors, who duly carried the cat from the eastern Mediterranean into western Europe. They were adopted enthusiastically by the Romans, who subsequently took them to India, and most likely also introduced them to China and Japan – cats accompanied imperial traders on the spice and silk routes from Europe through to Asia. In China and Japan, the cat came to earn its keep as the trusted protector of silk moth cocoons from the unwanted attentions of mice and other vermin. As such, the cat enjoyed a special privileged status in those societies, and especially in Japan where, highly unusually, it was taken up as a household animal long before the dog.

Dogs are a noticeable absence on Tashirojima, a tiny island an hour's ferry ride off the coast of central Ishinomaki City in Miyagi Prefecture, Japan. Humans are in the minority here, too, with the current, predominantly elderly, population standing at about one hundred people, the majority engaged in fishing. There are, however, estimated to be at least four times as many cats. These semi-feral creatures not only have the run of the place, but are honoured with their own shrine. Their every need is met by the island's residents, who believe the cats bring them good luck and actually saved the island from complete destruction when it was hit by the tsunami that followed the Tōhoku earthquake in 2011.

During the Edo period in Japan (1603–1868), silk and textile production rivalled fishing as Tashirojima's main industry and today's cats are direct descendants of the mousers brought over during that time. But with the emergence of improved synthetic fibres and a drift in fashion that moved away from traditional kimonos and toward more Western styles of dress, silk farming went into terminal decline across Japan in the 1970s. The end of silk farming was a major blow to the island's fortunes, and the number of its two-legged inhabitants fell accordingly, too. In the last decade, however, the felines have put Tashirojima on the tourist map, with ailurophiles flocking from all over the world to see 'cat island' and even to stay in one of the cat-themed chalets that can be rented in the summer months.

RIGHT: Visitors to Tashirojima can hire a 'kitty cabin' in which to stay (top), a design that suggests cats are revered above all else on this little island.

18° 56' 35.9" S 44° 47' 46.0" E

GRAND TSINGY

MADAGASCAR

Melaky

The fourth-largest island on Earth, Madagascar, off the southeastern coast of Africa, could almost be a whole lost continent. Developing at one remove from the rest of Eastern Africa – and on its own terms – it is the most biologically diverse island on the planet. Scientists have identified 200,000 different species on Madagascar, of which 75 per cent are found nowhere else on Earth. It is the only known natural habitat for the lemur, a furry teddy-bear-like prosimian with eyes bright as beads that currently holds the unenviable title of the world's most endangered primate. There remain eighty-five living species of lemur on Madagascar, in a variety of shapes, sizes and colours. The diminutive mouse lemur has the distinction of being the smallest primate on the planet. The John Cleese woolly lemur, or *Avahi cleesei*, was only discovered in a nature reserve in a remote part of the island in the 1990s. In 2005, the year this species was finally scientifically verified, it was named in honour of the long-legged star of *Monty Python* as a tribute to Cleese's contribution to raising awareness of their plight in the film *Fierce Creatures* and in his documentary *Operation Lemur with John Cleese*.

Eleven types of lemur live in Grand Tsingy – on the surface, seemingly one of the most inhospitable environs Madagascar has to offer. This massive 600 km² (230 sq mile) expanse of razor-sharp limestone pinnacles, some over 90 m (300 ft) high, is classified as 'the world's largest stone forest'. The word *tsingy* roughly translates as 'where one cannot walk', or 'place of walking on tiptoe'. It is a name that accurately describes the sheer impenetrability of the spiky terrain (it can take a day to negotiate 800 m/½ mile on foot), while reinforcing a local superstition that the stone forest, once the domain of evil spirits, is best left undisturbed.

Like most limestone, which forms in shallow, calm, warm marine waters, Grand Tsingy began life under the sea, some 200 million years ago, where a layer of calcite accrued to

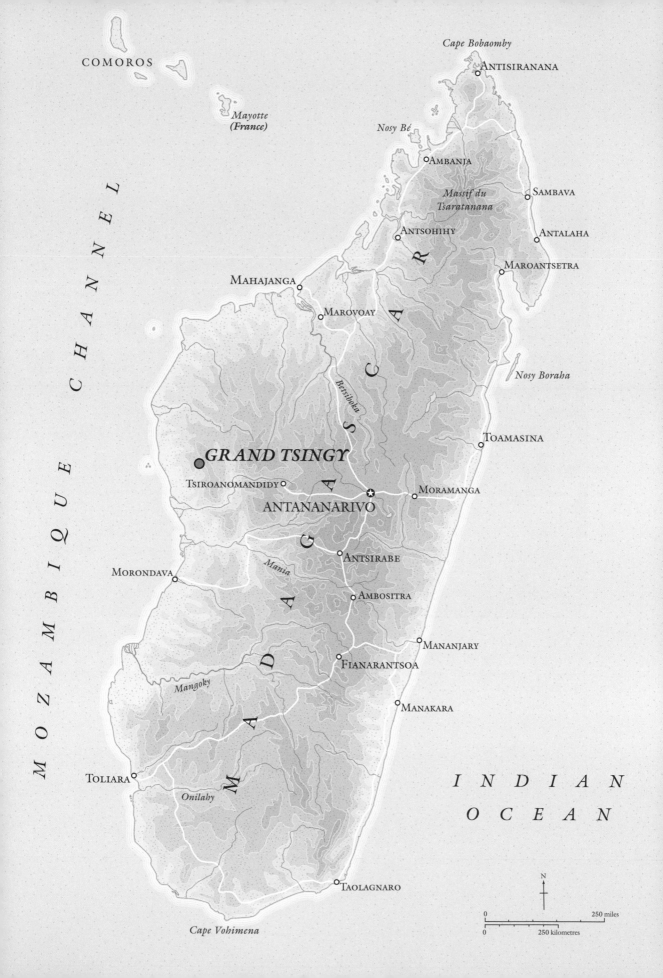

COMOROS

Mayotte
(France)

Cape Bobaomby

○ ANTISIRANANA

Nosy Bé

○ AMBANJA

Massif du Tsaratanana

○ SAMBAVA

○ ANTALAHA

○ ANTSOHIHY

□ MAROANTSETRA

○ MAHAJANGA

○ MAROVOAY

Nosy Boraha

M O Z A M B I Q U E   C H A N N E L

Betsiboka

○ TOAMASINA

GRAND TSINGY ●

○ TSIROANOMANDIDY

☆ ○ MORAMANGA

ANTANANARIVO

M A D A G A S C A R

○ ANTSIRABE

Mania

○ AMBOSITRA

○ MORONDAVA

○ MANANJARY

○ FIANARANTSOA

Mangoky

○ MANAKARA

TOLIARA ○

Onilahy

I N D I A N

O C E A N

○ TAOLAGNARO

Cape Vohimena

N

0 ——————— 250 miles

0 ——————— 250 kilometres

ABOVE: Visitors to Grand Tsingy can tread the well-worn boards of several rope bridges suspended high above the hostile terrain. At times the drop can be a dizzying 300 m (980 ft).

create a thick limestone bed. Tectonic activity, and the retreat of the ocean during the Pleistocene ice ages, brought this sedimentary rock to the surface. Tropical rains, lashing down for millions of monsoons, gradually dissolved the softer porous rock, leaving a porcupine-like landscape of tough, jagged stone quills. If forebidding to humans, Grand Tsingy – whose floor is amply potted with patches of dense vegetation – attracts a wider range of inhabitants than lemurs. The carnivorous falanouc, the ring-tailed mongoose, several bats, more than one hundred breeds of birds and forty-five species of reptile are all occupants of this vast dominion.

As one of the anthropologists who tracked down the *Avahi cleesei* observed, lemurs 'can't really walk'. Agile as cats, however, they love to jump from place to place and so this forest, with its columns of rock, store of leaves and berries to eat and physical isolation, is surprisingly conducive to sustaining the lives of these most imperilled of creatures.

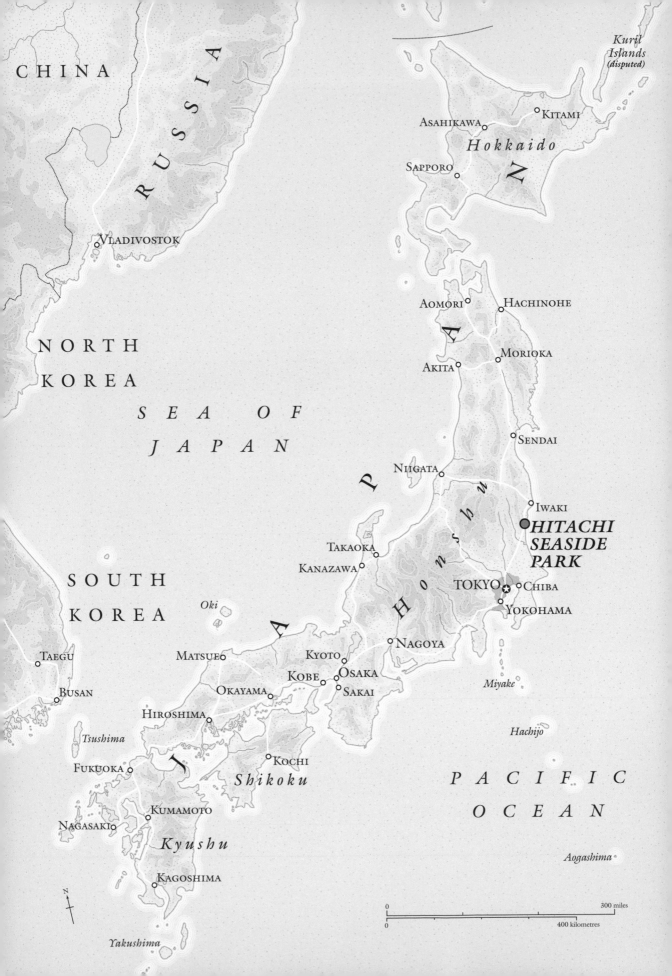

HITACHI SEASIDE PARK

JAPAN

Hitachinaka, Ibaraki

The Swedish botanist Carl Linnaeus is known as the father of taxonomy for devising the system for classification of all living organisms. In the 1740s, then the Professor of Medicine of Uppsala University, he became fascinated by the ways in which plants responded to the changing seasons of the year, even the cycles of individual days. Among his duties at the university (Scandinavia's oldest), was overseeing the upkeep of its botanical garden. His college rooms looked out onto the garden, and over the course of several years, he spent hours noting the minutest alterations in the plants. He saw how certain varieties opened and closed their flowers periodically, and recorded diurnal and seasonal variations from species to species. Using this data, he went on, in his 1751 treatise *Philosophia Botanica*, to propose the idea of a '*horologium florae*' or floral clock. This was to be an arrangement of particular herbs and flowers that might serve as a living, organic timepiece: horticulture, in effect, meeting horology, with the flora budding, blossoming and dying like clockwork. Linnaeus provided an illustration of how such a floral clock might look, but it is doubtful that he ever got round to planting one himself.

If, perhaps, not quite the place by which to set your watch, the Hitachi Seaside Park has a planting scheme worthy of Linnaeus nevertheless, where its seasonal shifts are among the most polychromatic of any garden in the world. In the Pacific coastal city of Hitachinaka in Japan's Ibaraki Prefecture, some two hours outside Tokyo, the park covers a sprawling 28 hectares (70 acres), its less verdant features including the usual seaside amusements of a ferris wheel, rollercoaster and putting green, along with a BMX track and cycle trails.

The vast flower gardens and meadows provide a calendar in colours; with millions of daffodils and 170 varieties of tulips contributing to its annual visual feast. Central to the park lies its great Miharashi Hill, which is crisscrossed by numerous paths offering fantastic views out onto the Pacific Ocean and down over the rest of the park. The hill is also the park's most colourful and chromatic attraction, since it is here that, from April to May, it turns a bright shade of eyeshadow-blue, its colour scheme outdoing the crystalline ocean of the nearby shore. In a botanical event referred to locally as '*Nemophila* Harmony' over 4.5 million *Nemophila* – or baby blue eyes – bloom on the hill's banks. At the other end of the year, in October, the hill's scores of *Kochia* bushes shift from emerald green to blazing red as the summer slips into autumn and the weather starts to cool. In such fashion, the changing of the seasons are shaded in, and the seeds of time sown to impressive effect.

BELOW: Summer at Hitachi Seaside Park, when the millions of delicate *Nemophila* flowers are in full bloom, stretching as far as the eye can see.

42° 45' 04.9" N 0° 30' 50.9" W

CANFRANC STATION

SPAIN

Canfranc

As destinations in themselves, or gateways to somewhere else, railway stations contain imaginative possibilities as much as journey-weary passengers. A station can be a statement of intent, the laying of a new line an invitation to take a trip into the unknown – or, at the very least to the next town.

Canfranc promised to be something bigger; a bridge between two nations, and the culmination of a bold project involving much tunnelling through the hard rock of mountains to open up Franco-Spanish travel and trade. Perched high up in the Pyrenees, on the Spanish side of the border with France, its architecture was late art nouveau on the grandest scale. The station's opening in 1928, attended by the French President Gaston Doumergue and Spanish King Alfonso XIII, was large and lavish. The platforms were over 200 m (650 ft) long, the second longest ever laid in Europe, and the main building boasted 365 windows – one for each day of the year, for reasons that remain mysterious – and hundreds of doors; all of this to serve a mountainside village of just five hundred.

Any transnational voyagers who came through were forced to change trains here, owing to differing rail gauges. Little wonder, then, that it was nicknamed the 'Titanic of the Mountains'. After the Wall Street Crash of 1929, the station was widely predicted to sink without trace, with as few as fifty passengers a day gracing its concourses. Closed down by Franco for a brief period at the height of the Spanish Civil War, once the line reopened its trains served as an escape route for Jews fleeing fascism and as a conduit for Allied espionage during the Second World War. The railway was also commandeered by the Nazis. Although operational in the postwar period, the line lacked due care and the station began to fall into disrepair (although it was thought to have served as a set by David Lean in his 1965 movie adaptation of Boris Pasternak's epic Russian novel *Doctor Zhivago* – a claim that has since

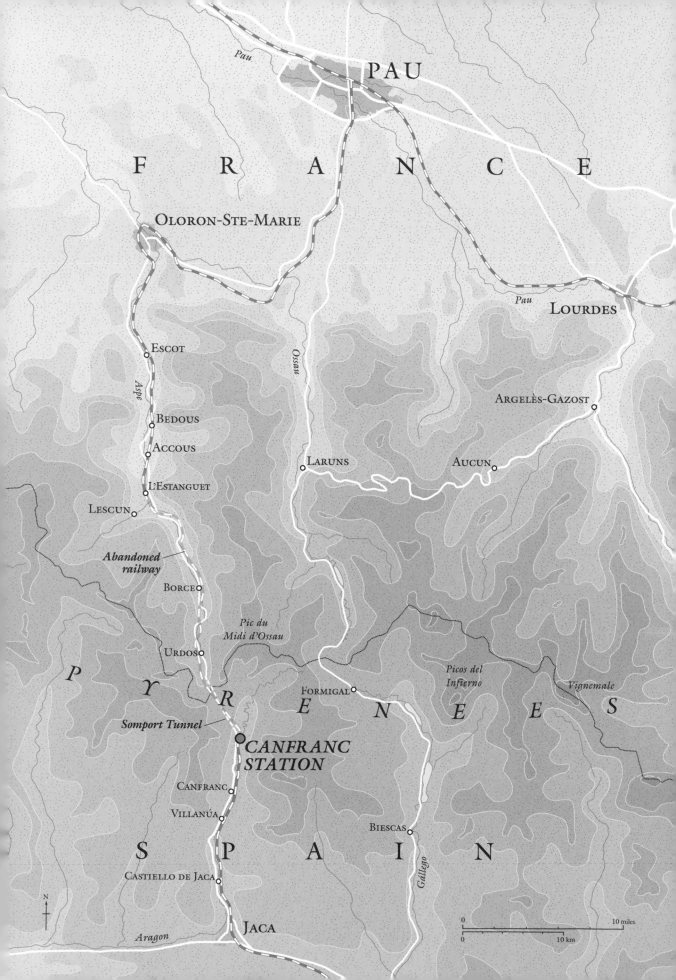

been disputed). The station finally closed in 1970, when a train derailed, damaging the track on the French side. Abandoned, it was left to the mercy of vandals, who daubed its walls with graffiti and smashed up its ticket hall.

In recent years, the local government in Aragon purchased the station, patched up its roof and plans to refurbish it as a hotel-station complex, relaunching rail travel through the Pyrenees. French counterparts in Bordeaux also support the scheme and it has been blessed with the promise of financial backing from the European Union in Brussels. At present a modest service of two local trains a day run nearby, but the original station remains a beautiful ruin, poised between an elegant, if slightly ignominious, past and a still uncertain future.

ABOVE: While Canfranc station awaits its return to former glory, operators offer guided hard-hat tours of the grand lobby within. Outside on the tracks sits a rusting train, once part of the line's fleet.

SELECTED BIBLIOGRAPHY

This publication owes an enormous debt to numerous other books and articles. This select bibliography will, hopefully, give credit where credit is due and point those who want to know more in the right direction.

- Allegro, John M. *The Dead Sea Scrolls*, Penguin, Harmondsworth, 1957

- Aujoulat, Norbert. *The Splendour of Lascaux: Rediscovering the Greatest Treasure of Prehistoric Art*, Thames & Hudson, London, 2005

- Baker, Mark; Fallon, Steve. *Romania & Bulgaria*, Lonely Planet Guides, Footscray, Victoria, 2013

- Beuke, Mary Beth. *The Ultimate Guide to Sea Glass: Beach Comber's Edition: Finding, Collecting, Identifying, and Using the Oceans Most Beautiful Stones*, Skyhorse Publishing, Delaware, 2016

- Bloomfield, Andrew. *Call of the Cats: What I Learned About Life and Love from a Feral Colony*, New World Library, Novato, California, 2016

- Box, Ben. *Cuzco, La Paz & Lake Titicaca*, Robert and Daisy Kunstaetter, Footprint, Bath, 2011

- Brooks, Christopher. *Black Rock Desert*, Arcadia Publishing: Images of America, Charleston, South Carolina, 2013

- Brown, Alfred Gordon. *Madeira: A Concise Guide for the Visitor*, Union-Castle Mail Steamship Co., London, 1951

- Brown, Roslind Varghese; Spilling, Michael. *Tunisia; Cultures of the World*, Cavendish Square Publishing, London, 2008

- Coarelli, Filippo, et al. *Pompeii*, Riverside, New York; David & Charles, Newton Abbott, 2002

- Ciarallo, Annamaria, De Carolis, Ernesto, eds. *Around the Walls of Pompeii: the Ancient City in its Natural Environment*, Electa, Milan, 1998

- Correia, Mariana; Dipasquale, Letizia; Mecca, Saverio, eds. *VERSUS: Heritage for Tomorrow*: *Vernacular Knowledge for Sustainable Architecture*, Firenze University Press, Firenze, 2014

- Chrystal, Paul. *Secret Knaresborough*, Amberley, Stroud, 2014

- Darke, Diana. *Eastern Turkey*, Bradt Travel Guides, Chalfont St. Peter, 2014

- Dolson, Hildergarde. *They Struck Oil: The Gaudy and Turbulent Years of the First Oil Rush: Pennsylvania 1859–1880*, Hammond, Hammond & Co, London, 1959

- Darwin, Charles. *The Origin of Species and the Voyage of the Beagle*, Vintage Classics, London, 2009

- Eisenberg, Azriel Louis. *The Great Discovery: the Story of the Dead Sea Scrolls*, Abelard-Schuman London, New York, 1957

- Elliot, W. R. *Monemvasia: The Gibraltar of Greece*, Dobson, London, 1971

- Elborough, Travis. *A Walk in the Park: The Life and Times of a People's Institution*, Jonathan Cape, London, 2016

- Farrow John; Farrow, Susan. *Madeira: the Complete Guide*, Hale, London, 1990, 1994

- Gillespie, Rosemary G; Clague, David. *Encyclopedia of Islands*, University of California Press: Oakland, 2009

- Gillon, Jack; Parkinson, Fraser. *Leith: Through Time*, Amberley Publishing, Stroud, 2014

- Gunn, John, ed. *Encyclopedia of Caves and Karst Science*, Routledge, London, 2004

- Grant, K. Thalia; B. Estes, Gregory. *Darwin in Galápagos: Footsteps to a New World*, Princeton University Press, Princeton, N.J., 2009

- Graves, Robert. *The Greek Myths*, Penguin Books, Harmondsworth, 1955

- Grandin, Greg. *Fordlandia: The Rise and Fall of Henry Ford's Forgotten Jungle City*, Icon, London, 2010

- Hadden, Peter. *North New Zealand: A Natural History of the Upper North Island*, Wairau Press, Random House, Auckland, 2014

- Harris, David. *Sierra Leone: A Political History*, Hurst & Company, London, 2013

- Hess, John. *The Galápagos: Exploring Darwin's Tapestry*, University of Missouri Press, Columbia, MO; London, 2009

- Howse, Christopher. *The Train in Spain*, Continuum/Bloomsbury, London, 2013

- Kalder, Daniel. *Lost Cosmonaut: Travels to the Republics that Tourism Forgot*, Faber and Faber, London, 2006

- Kalligas, Charis A. *Monemvasia: A Byzantine City State*, Routledge, London; New York, 2010

- Jorgensen, Anna; Keenan, Richard, eds. *Urban Wildscapes*, Routledge Abingdon, UK; New York, 2012

- Krajeski, Jenna. 'Death in Garbage City', *The New Yorker* magazine, 9 March 2011

- Lebow, Katherine. *Unfinished Utopia: Nowa Huta, Stalinism, and Polish Society, 1949–56*, Cornell University Press, Ithaca, New York, 2013

- Leffman, David, et al. *The Rough Guide to China*, Rough Guides, London, 2017

- Marriott, James; Minio-Paluello, Mika. *The Oil Road: Journeys from the Caspian Sea to the City of London*, Verso, London, 2012

- Mayson, Richard. *Madeira: The Islands and their Wines*, Infinite Ideas, Oxford, 2015

- Morritt, Hope. *Rivers of Oil: The Founding of North America's Petroleum Industry*, Quarry Press, Kingston, Ontario, 1993

- Nairn, Ian. *Nairn's London*, Penguin Classics, London, 2015

- Nicholls, Henry. *The Galápagos: A Natural History*, Profile Books Ltd, London, 2014

- Nicholson, Geoff. *Walking in Ruins*, Harbour Books, Bath, 2013

- Packham, Chris, foreword by. *Natural Wonders of the World*, Dorling Kindersley Limited, London, 2017

- Panetta, Marisa Ranieri, ed. *Pompeii: The History, Life and Art of the Buried City*, White Star Publishers, Novara, Italy, 2012

- Pauketat, Timothy R. *Cahokia: Ancient America's Great City on the Mississippi*, Viking, New York, 2009

- Pohlen, Jerome. *Oddball Florida: A Guide to Some Really Strange Places*, Chicago Review Press, Chicago, IL., Gazelle, Lancaster, 2003

- Raffaele, Paul. *Among the Cannibals: Adventures on the Trail of Man's Darkest Ritual*, Smithsonian Books, Collins, New York, 2008

- Reader's Digest. *Discovering the Wonders of our World*, Reader's Digest Association, London, 1993

- Ruspoli, Mario, translated from the French by Sebastian Wormell. *The Cave of Lascaux: The Final Photographic Record*, Thames and Hudson, London, 1987

- Russell, David Lee. *Oglethorpe and Colonial Georgia: A History, 1733–1783*, McFarland & Co., Jefferson, NC; London, 2006

- Sanders, Don and Susan. *The American Drive-In Movie Theatre*, Motorbooks International, St. Paul, MN, Sparkford, Haynes, 2003

- Sayre, Roger. *From Space to Place: An Image Atlas of World Heritage Sites on the 'in Danger' List*, World Heritage Series, UNESCO Publishing, Paris, France, 2012

- Schama, Simon. *Rough Crossings: Britain, the Slaves and the American Revolution*, BBC Books, London, 2006

- Snow, Richard. *I Invented the Modern Age: The rise of Henry Ford*, Scribner, New York, 2013

- Stewart, Paul D. *Galápagos: The Islands that Changed the World*, BBC Books, London, 2006

- Stoneman, Richard. *A Traveller's History of Turkey*, Armchair Traveller, London, 2011

- Thornton, Ian. *Darwin's islands: A Natural History of the Galápagos*, Natural History Press, New York, 1971

- Twitchell, James B. *Winnebago Nation: The RV in American Culture*, Columbia University Press, New York, 2014

- Velton, Ross. *Mali*, Bradt Travel Guides, Chalfont St. Peter, 2009

- Vermes, Geza. *The Story of the Scrolls: The Miraculous Discovery and True Significance of the Dead Sea Scrolls*, Penguin, London; New York, 2010

- Walker, Brett L. *A Concise History of Japan*, Cambridge University Press, Cambridge, 2015

- Welsh, Irvine. *The Blade Artist*, Jonathan Cape, London, 2016

- Welsh, Irvine. *Trainspotting*, Minerva, London, 1994

- Wheeler, Tony. *Papua New Guinea: A Travel Survival Kit*, Lonely Planet, Hawthorn, Vic.; London, 1993

- Wilson, Thomas D. *The Oglethorpe Plan: Enlightenment Design in Savannah and Beyond*, University of Virginia Press, Charlottesville, 2015

- Windels, Fernand. *The Lascaux Cave Paintings*, Faber and Faber, London, 1959

- Windsor, Diana. *Mother Shipton's Prophecy Book: The Story of her Life and her Most Famous Prophecies*, Mother Shipton's Cave Ilex Leisure Ltd, Knaresborough, 1996

- Young, Biloine Whiting; Fowler, Melvin J. *Cahokia: The Great Native American Metropolis*, University of Illinois Press,Urbana, 1999

ACKNOWLEDGEMENTS

Thanks, first, to my editor Lucy Warburton for supplying the concept for this sequel of sorts to the *Atlas of Improbable Places*, and Anna Southgate who diligently copy-edited the text that emerged as a result of that brief.

Thanks to the staff and librarians at The British Library in St Pancras and The London Library in St James's and Hackney Libraries, Stoke Newington branch.

And in addition I'd like to thank, friends, ancient and modern, my folks and family on either side of the Atlantic and my beautiful and brilliant wife, Emily Bick.

The Publisher would like to thank Collective Architecture for assistance with images for Leith Fort, a project developed by The City of Edinburgh Council and Port of Leith Housing Association with architects Collective Architecture and Malcolm Fraser Architects.

PICTURE CREDITS

INDEX

Brimming with creative inspiration, how-to projects and useful information to enrich your everyday life, Quarto Knows is a favourite destination for those pursuing their interests and passions. Visit our site and dig deeper with our books into your area of interest: Quarto Creates, Quarto Cooks, Quarto Homes, Quarto Lives, Quarto Drives, Quarto Explores, Quarto Gifts, or Quarto Kids.

First published in 2018 by White Lion Publishing,
an imprint of The Quarto Group
The Old Brewery,
6 Blundell Street
London N7 9BH
United Kingdom

www.QuartoKnows.com

ISBN 978 1 78131 716 7
Ebook ISBN 978 1 78131 839 3

10 9 8 7 6 5 4 3 2 1
2022 2021 2020 2019 2018

Designed by Ashley Western

Printed in Slovenia by GPS Group

FSC
www.fsc.org
MIX
Paper from responsible sources
FSC® C110418

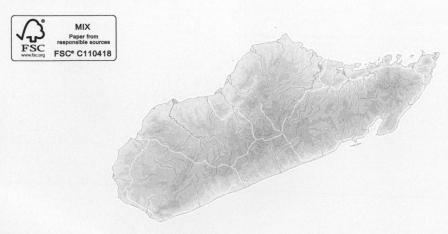